Advance Praise for
Through Dangerous Doors: A Life at Risk

Through Dangerous Doors is an engaging and snappily written reflection on a life charted by risk. Like the dangerous mountains he eventually comes to climb, Lee's need to be on the edge and in the flow guide him on a fascinating ascent up the American socio-economic pyramid, a challenging mountain in itself, and geographically from the lowland South to high country of the North. Small wonder that when Lee and his wife arrive in Calgary, Alberta, to live for a decade they immerse themselves in what Lee wisely comes to realize is one of the most dangerous, yet spiritually rewarding mountain ranges in the world—the Canadian Rockies. Lee's lifelong evaluation, and refinement of, the risk versus reward calculation is educational. And I love the way he calls poppycock when he sees it. Lee shares life lessons that were hard won and valuable to all.

—Barry Blanchard, UIAGM/IFMGA Mountain Guide, author of *The Calling—A Life Rocked by Mountains,* winner of the Boardman-Tasker Prize for Mountain Literature

Much more than a book on mountaineering, Robert Charles Lee's memoir delves deeply into the relationship between risk and reward, exploring the things we can control and those we can't. His journey of self-discovery has resulted in a thoughtful meditation on the nature of adventure and what makes for a life well lived. Lee's story will resonate with any readers who have experienced the incomparable satisfaction of challenging themselves while at the same time understanding the wisdom of respecting their limits.

—Scott Zesch, author of *The Captured,* winner of the TCU Texas Book Award

This is a memoir like few others, in that the author is intent on beseeching his readers not to follow the example of his own life. The story he tells shows that this is very good advice indeed, but nevertheless his tale of improbable escapes from one looming disaster after another is both instructive and entertaining.

—William Leiss, Queen's University, author of: *In the Chamber of Risks: Understanding Risk Controversies, Mad Cows and Mother's Milk: The Perils of Poor Risk Communication,* and *Risk and Responsibility.*

In this engaging and very readable memoir, Robert Lee reminds us that life IS risk. Humans only continue to learn, grow and evolve through facing and conquering risks. Whether the risks are involuntary or voluntary, Lee aptly emphasizes that the key to survival, or even thriving, is how we choose to understand and manage those risks. While Lee's recounting of his numerous climbing risk adventures reflects his personal approach to risk and risk management, his stories will resonate strongly with anyone who seeks the challenge and stimulation of being a 'risk taker'. This book will ultimately make you examine more closely your own life in relation to the risks you choose or don't choose to undertake.

—Cindy Jardine, University of the Fraser Valley, world record skydiver

As autobiographies like *Educated* and *The Glass Castle* have taught us, growing up through hardship can be remarkably annealing. So too in this disarmingly honest memoir, where Lee relates his annealed response. He adeptly strings us along his extraordinary lifepath from childhood until retirement using an idiosyncratic lens: A meditation on risk serves as Lee's throughline, one informed by his career in risk analysis. Sit and enjoy the windfall of a raconteur relaying how he and his fellow travelers have encountered and responded to risks. Many encounters, like his vivid recounts of ice and mountain climbing, are quite intense. We get a taste of life as a forester, psychedelic-explorer, musician, academic, blessed husband and alpinist. Some entrancing events, nicely infused with a humble "stock-taking" of the cards that were dealt, and the choices made. An extraordinary story that resonates beyond risk.

—Kevin Brand, University of Ottawa

"Life is either a daring adventure or nothing at all" wrote Helen Keller in her passageway focused book *The Open Door*. Metaphorical passageways hurtle us in and out of the risky exploits of Mr. Lee in *Through Dangerous Doors*. Climbing on a glacier or rappelling down a mountain, Lee shows us the thrill of daring adventure. But risk is not the goal, it is the price paid for adventure—and sometimes that price is too high. Lee helps us see that managing risk, sometimes with tools or technology and sometimes by knowing when to say no, is the key to continuing to be able to pass through new doors.

—George Gray, George Washington University, co-author of *Risk: A Practical Guide for Deciding What's Really Safe and What's Really Dangerous in the World Around You*

Through Dangerous Doors

A Life at Risk

Robert Charles Lee

E. L. Marker
Salt Lake City

E. L. Marker, an imprint of WiDō Publishing
Salt Lake City, Utah
www.widopublishing.com

Cover design by Steve Novak
Book design by Marny K. Parkin

Cover photo (front material photo credit):
A happy risk scientist on the summit of Mt. Hermit, British Columbia. Shortly after Linda took this photo, we were almost zapped by lightning (credit: L. Cook).

ISBN: 978-1-947966-45-1

To Linda,
who shelters me from the storm

Contents

Raison D'être

Driving to the edge
Of today or tomorrow
It makes no difference to me

Walking to the edge
Whether spacious or narrow
It makes no difference to me

Climbing to the edge
Of ecstasy or sorrow
It makes no difference to me

The crux is the edge
It moves me to the marrow
This makes a difference to me

The edge aligns me
The edge defines me
I have no resistance
To the edge of existence

Prelude

RISK DEFINES MY LIFE. I'VE OPENED MANY DANGEROUS DOORS FOR the rewards, and closed some. These doors profoundly affect my views of myself and the world. I've been subject to a wide spectrum of involuntary risks as well.

I'm also a former risk scientist who studied and applied risk assessment and management for more than a quarter century in a wide range of disciplines. The main life lesson I've learned is even though I may be subject to or even addicted to risky situations, I can manage risk if I stay rational.

Risk has different meanings to different people. To a scientist like myself, it's a function of both probability or chance, and consequences. Some risks are involuntary or imposed upon us, and some are voluntary. The consequences are often negative, involving losses such as injury or death, but risk can also lead to great rewards. My life involves an ongoing personal calculus balancing reward and loss.

Publishing this memoir may be perilous, as I reveal much about myself and others. I use pseudonyms for everyone except myself, my parents, my wife, and public figures. I represent dialogue to the best of my recollection. Otherwise, this memoir is fact-checked and accurate to the highest degree possible. I found my journey worthwhile, but I *do not* suggest anyone else should open such dangerous doors.

If the doors of perception were cleansed, everything would appear to man as it is: Infinite. For man has closed himself up, till he sees things thro' narrow chinks of his cavern.
    —William Blake

There are only three sports: bullfighting, motor racing, and mountaineering; all the rest are merely games.
    —Attributed to Ernest Hemingway

. . . you have to be good when you take nasty risks, or you'll lose it, and then you're in serious trouble.
    —Dr. Hunter S. Thompson

I'm climbing higher mountains, trying to get home.
    —Traditional gospel song

First Movement:
Solo (1957 to 1987)

The Free-Range Door

THE HORSE GALLOPS ACROSS OUR RANGE OF A FEW ACRES. I'M EXHILARATED and barely hanging on, but my father, Charles, is watching. I go hunting with him, and he guffaws when I'm almost knocked flat by the recoil of my first deafening discharge of a twelve-gauge. I explore the copperhead-snake, wasp, hornet, tick, chigger, and poison ivy infested hardwood forest on our property. My feet and legs are bare much of the year. However, I tread carefully. The door to the outdoors opens. I'm six or seven years old, but I eagerly enter.

☙

I was serious about managing risk, even as a kid. Life began as a late Boomer and a Fallout Boy. A B-52 bomber broke up over my home state in 1961, releasing two nuclear bombs. Above-ground nuclear weapons tests were conducted in the United States West, creating radioactive dust clouds. These events perhaps foretold a career steeped in radiation.

My family is of working-class, British and Scots-Irish ancestry; the original hillbillies in the Appalachians and Piedmont. My birthplace and time were subject to systemic White racism, resulting in the designation "Klansville, USA." We lived near Salisbury in rural Granite Quarry, North Carolina, about a mile from the gated compound of Bob Jones, a powerful Ku Klux Klan Grand Dragon. Jones was kicked out of the Navy for refusing to salute a Black officer, proclaiming, "I won't salute no nigger." Jones helped expand the North Carolina KKK to over ten-thousand members. A friend and I once snuck over to watch a cross-burning near his property.

If the neighborhood White men weren't pickin' and grinnin', drinking and playing guitars and banjos on their porches on a Saturday night, they were hanging out with their bros in the local men's Klub. I don't recall any lynchings, but harassment and violence were common. The county sheriff was a Klan member, and wore a Western cowboy hat on his bald head and a patch over one dead eye. Chain-gangs broke rocks in the steaming Southern heat under the squinty eyes of shotgun-toting overseers on horseback. Most of the Black people in the area lived in segregation in the equivalent of a shanty town. Schools, churches, and most activities were segregated.

My family is purported to be related to the slaveowner and traitor General Robert E. Lee, but I've not been able to verify this. If true, I'm appalled in a moral sense, but there's nothing I can do about it aside from trying to be an anti-racist and a good citizen. At least I don't have the same middle name. I do indeed have a red neck, but solely due to years of outdoor activity.

My father, Charles, was no stranger to risk. He served as a United States Marine drill sergeant and war dog trainer in World War II. He was a marksman, boxer, expert swimmer, hunter, hunting dog trainer, fisherman, and horseman. As far as I can tell, he was good at whatever he tackled. He was a so-called "good ol' boy," but he was intelligent and wasn't racist, which was itself risky in a racist society. He was raised in rural North Carolina and loved the outdoors. His brothers were also intelligent and interested in the natural world. Charles was a small-time homebuilder by profession, which had its dangers. He was struck by lightning once while working on the roof of a house and tumbled off, breaking his leg.

My mother, Frances, was the flaming red-haired, seventh daughter of a quarryman and his wife from Leicestershire, England. This resulted in unusual speech patterns and word usage for a Southern boy. I loved going to her father Pop's cottage to visit. It was a pat of working-class, Old Blighty butter in a sea of hick grits.

Frances wasn't as risk-seeking as Charles, but she loved him and indulged his lifestyle. Charles was a strong advocate of what's now called free-range parenting, but he made sure the kids applied some common sense. My free-range childhood was the start of a long and winding road to rational risk management.

The family likely lived below the federal poverty level, but we grew vegetables, and hunted and fished for meat. I'm not sure whether we were called "White trash" or not. We lived in a small frame house Charles built, so we weren't trailer trash. Charles was the alpha over the other five humans, a couple of horses, a dozen or so hunting hounds, several pet dogs and cats, a cow, chickens, and various wild animals we kids caught and eventually released. All those kids and animals required food, so this contributed to our poverty. I didn't inherit Charles's horse addiction, but my older sister did, and horses became the focus of her life. All the kids loved and still love dogs, the noblest of beasts.

Being an ex-Marine and a natural teacher, Charles taught the kids how to fight and shoot as early as possible. Marines specialize in those skills and consider them important. Part of the reason may have been a practical risk management strategy, given our family didn't belong to the Klan tribe. These were dangerous times for Blacks, and to a lesser degree, Whites who didn't buy into the systemic and often violent racism extant in the South.

Hunting was another reason for early firearms training. Charles owned a half dozen or so hunting rifles and shotguns he kept unlocked in open racks in our home. He kept unlocked guns on a rack in his pickup truck, as did many men. We would never have considered touching Charles's guns without his permission. He taught us how to hunt and take care of guns as soon as we could pick them up. I received a twenty-two caliber rifle and a twenty-gauge shotgun of my own around the age of seven.

Packs of feral dogs prowled the countryside. Many families let their dogs roam, and didn't neuter them. Chickens and other small animals were at risk from these packs, and occasionally the neighborhood men went dog hunting. Dog- and cockfighting were common, but my parents disapproved.

Charles never used physical punishment on me, unlike Frances, who later in life didn't spare the rod. He was a powerful man, but I don't recall seeing him pissed, or even in a bad mood. According to older relatives, he was hilarious, although I was too young to fully appreciate it. He referred to me as an "odd liddle feller," an assessment that was and still is, accurate.

I was born left-handed. Back then, southpaw-ness was considered a mental and physical defect. Schools encouraged right-handedness, and Frances proclaimed, "I won't have any left-handers in my house." The basis for this policy was unclear, as were many of her stances. The sinister implications of being a lefty were never clear to me. I was hampered as an athlete until I ignored Frances and switched to using my left hand for throwing and other boyish activities. I still have unreadable, right-handed penmanship, but using the left would be worse.

A rural Southern accent is often associated with sub-normal intellect, bigotry, and other negative attributes. Many years ago, a dear, sweet Yankee friend from the North commented, "I'm amazed you became an academician, having such an accent." At the time, I hadn't lived in the South for twenty years. She had no idea this observation might be insulting or condescending. I've known others from the South to tamp down or discard their Southern accents due to negative perceptions, which ain't easy. I never cared enough to bother, but my yokel-ish accent may have hampered my life in subtle ways.

Our family always made a yearly trip to the Appalachian Mountains, often in the fall when the hardwood forest blazed with color. A surefire way to tell somebody ain't from around there is if they pronounce Appalachia with a long *a* sound on the third vowel. Our activities were largely limited to driving around, in the spirit of the 1950s and early 1960s. However, there were high points for an odd liddle feller. I wore a favorite sweater which I imagined to be my special protective mountain parka. Charles gave me an old masonry hammer I employed as an ice ax in mountain climbing fantasies when we stopped for breaks. This foreshadowed the pursuits that have consumed much of my adult life.

Once, the family was in the middle of a sketchy suspension bridge with big air underneath, between the two peaks of Grandfather Mountain, North Carolina. Charles started to swing the bridge back and forth, to the kids' glee and Frances's terror. To this day, I try to swing my wife, Linda, on any swingable bridge, but she demands I go across first. I'm my father's child in many ways.

I called my parents "Mommy" and "Daddy" when I was liddle, but for reasons unclear, I started using their first names as a youth. Perhaps I was trying to distance myself from my mother, for reasons that will become clear. She also suffered a number of silly and obscure nicknames, including *Chewie,* which I don't think was short for Chewbacca. I may have called her Frances just to be different.

My father died when I was eight, the year the Civil Rights Act passed. He died in his forties, victim of a hereditary kidney disease called glomerulonephritis, which skipped his sons due to genetic luck. The loss of my father plunged me into a maelstrom of involuntary risk.

Frances was a fine mother and partner to Charles when he was alive, but after he died, she was forced to work. She'd never worked in a formal job but had taken secretarial training at a junior college. She sold off most of the animals, Charles's guns, a rental house he'd built, and most possessions of value. I doubt the family had any savings. Frances was unprepared for working and single parenthood, in both temperament and practical matters, so she hired a Black woman named Annie to babysit us and run the household. She was "the help."

My two oldest siblings started to grow wild, but Annie kept me and my younger brother under control. She was a hefty, strong, and competent woman, somebody you didn't want to mess with. As long as she commanded our respect, we continued to live a similar lifestyle as before.

Annie influenced my musical brain in the form of gospel and soul music she listened to on Black radio stations. I thought it was cool, and I enjoyed seeing her sway to the grooves and hearing her sing along. Later, when I became a musician, I appreciated how rare it is for music to speak from the depths of the soul.

While Charles was alive, the family attended both Lutheran and Episcopal churches, according to the preferences of my parents. The existence of two different Christian denominations in one small, rural town was due to settlement by immigrant quarrymen of German and British descent. I found the churches and their teachings interesting. They represented two interpretations of the same mythology, and I enjoyed some of the music.

After Charles died, though, I told Frances I didn't believe any of the spiritual stuff. She was indifferent, so I backslid. I never saw any value in supernatural belief. Lack of belief was associated with risk, if I gave any credence to Blaise Pascal's wager for the existence of a god or gods. I didn't, and eternal damnation was and remains the absolute least of my worries. Much later though, I came to appreciate Pascal as a father of decision analysis.

Frances slipped into clinical depression and an anxiety disorder. She was deeply in love with Charles, and unprepared for working and raising four large, headstrong, and unruly kids. Frances did her best, but she wasn't a strong woman. She was broken, and for years, was prescribed a bewildering cocktail of powerful and toxic drugs. It wasn't until she was in her sixties that she was weaned off the drugs and her condition stabilized. Her eventual dementia could be partially attributed to drug use. Many elderly people take multiple prescription and nonprescription drugs, unaware of possible negative interactions. If they drink alcohol as well, they risk increased psychological and physical damage.

Modern medicine is miraculous, but it doesn't always work as well as it should. My health risks due to medical errors increased. This has been a major source of involuntary risk throughout my life. The first I remember was a prescription error. We lived in a rural area with many species of grass which flowered much of the year, and I developed a severe grass pollen allergy. Our physician, who still had bathrooms labeled *Men*, *Women*, and *Colored*, as if the latter were a third gender, prescribed one-hundred milligram capsules of diphenhydramine (Benadryl) every few hours, the maximum recommended adult dose. Diphenhydramine is also used as a sleep aid. I was a child zombie as a result. Perhaps Frances found me more manageable when I was zombie-fied. I missed much of the second grade because I simply couldn't think. I don't remember when the dose was adjusted downward, but due to a lack of other effective antihistamines, I took diphenhydramine for years.

I compensated for the zombie-ness by self-medicating with large amounts of sugary and caffeine-laden soda, and sugar in general. This didn't help my oral hygiene, and had other adverse effects. In grade school, fluoride treatment was made available. Without it, I could've been indentured by now. Fluoride was also added to toothpaste (*Look, Mom, no cavities!*). The result of the overuse of fluoride was mild fluorosis, manifesting as whiter spots on my teeth. A dentist from my childhood, whom I recall with clarity because he had unpleasantly large and hairy, ungloved fingers, tried to grind away the spots on my incisors until he realized they weren't just on the surface.

I don't recall flossing until I was a young adult. The family had no dental insurance, contributing to decay and crooked, White-trash teeth. Only wealthier kids received good dental care and braces. It's surprising I still have the roots of all my teeth.

A missed childhood diagnosis was myopia, which isn't a sudden onset condition. My third-grade teacher finally alerted Frances to the fact I couldn't see a damn thing. Being able to see clearly with prescription lenses opened doors to many new worlds.

Frances loved to read, and she had a small library including a complete set of encyclopedias, which I read often. I read the entire King James Bible, as well as Greek, Roman, Norse, and other mythologies. I read everything I could find. I read the dictionary when I couldn't find anything else. All this reading was a positive thing. Rural Southern schools back then weren't exactly paragons of learning. History and social studies curricula were laughable, especially with regard to slavery and racism. "Fake news" isn't a new invention. My voracious reading balanced the risks associated with a poor education, which can persist throughout life.

Back then, a Southern boy who didn't play football, baseball, or basketball was considered a lower phylum of life. Confused hand dominance impeded my sports ability, but I also wore glasses and did well in academics. I was therefore branded as a nerd, a significant psychological and social impediment. These days, it's cool to be a nerd, but certainly not then. I was excluded from the athletes' tribe, and always picked last for teams.

This was devastating, but perhaps fortunate. There's no better way to put a kid at risk for a lifetime of physical pain and dysfunction than to let them engage in contact team sports. Once I shifted to left-handed athletic activities, I became more proficient in baseball and softball. This was bad enough, considering the risk of high-speed balls hitting sensitive parts of the body such as the nuts and noggin. I wore a cup, but good batting helmets weren't common when I played Little League baseball. My left shoulder and elbow suffered from throwing hard with poor form and little muscle. I was never good in true contact sports such as basketball or football, which was fortunate. Kids are at much greater risk for injury playing these sports.

The risks added up. Many were then uncertain, at least among the general public, such as health effects associated with tobacco use. One way to make a little money during the season was *pulling*, or harvesting, tobacco, a major crop in North Carolina. I started work before the age of ten, toiling alongside mostly Black adult laborers. Between sweating bullets in the torrid Carolina climate and getting tobacco plant sap all over my hands and arms, I recall being quite buzzed. The nicotine in the 'baccy countered my diphenhydramine zombie-ness. Most of the adult men, including Charles, smoked and chewed tobacco, as did many boys. The rate of lung and oral cancer must have been whopping. Chewie refused to kiss Charles until he spit out his chewbacca. I chewed 'baccy once I started playing Little League. All the boys did. If they didn't enjoy it, they chewed to avoid being ostracized. It's surprising I never became addicted, although there's likely a genetic component to tobacco addiction.

It's impossible to estimate my personal cumulative risk associated with all the toxic stuff I was exposed to in the 1950s and 1960s. I'm uncertain exactly what I was exposed to or in what amounts. Environmental protection regulations didn't exist, and food safety was rudimentary. The family lived on the edge of the higher radon zone in North Carolina, on top of granite with radioactive minerals as part of its composition. Our house was ridden with asbestos, including the siding and flooring, and perhaps the roofing and insulation. Lead from gasoline and paint was everywhere, as were numerous other chemicals later banned. Many substances later found to be toxic existed in prepared foods at the time.

I begged for and received a chemistry set for Christmas one year and proceeded to alchemize foul and toxic-fumed concoctions. I used an asbestos heat-diffusing pad over my Bunsen burner when boiling these brews. I melted lead, because it was interesting to transform a metal to liquid. I soldered wires in old electronic equipment, resulting in more lead fume exposure and potential electrocution. I tried to make gunpowder, but only succeeded in exposing myself to choking smoke. We burned most of our trash in old oil barrels, and I threw in objects or substances that exploded or caused fireballs or stunk. I collected mercury from old switches, thermometers, and other sources, acquiring a fat marble-size ball to play with. As a junior rockhound, I collected radioactive uranium minerals found in North Carolina pegmatite.

I explored under the house and in old abandoned buildings contaminated with pesticides. Frances didn't let us ride our bikes behind the dichlorodiphenyltrichloroethane, or DDT-fogging trucks patrolling the streets during mosquito season, like many other neighborhood kids. Although DDT *per se* wasn't likely to be particularly toxic to the kids, at least in an acute sense, I'm not sure what organic solvent mixture was employed to dissolve the insecticide. Multiple solvents were often used, some of which were nasty. Any one of these chemical risks may not have been of particular concern, but cumulative risk should have been. Whether these experiences started me down the road to a career in toxicology, is lost in the pesticidal fog of history.

I still owned firearms. There were no shooting ranges. I just went out into the woods or a field and blew away inanimate objects. Good thing there were no passersby. I had an aversion to shooting animals, if not humans. I engaged in BB gun wars with neighbor kids, which seemed safer than using a shotgun. Nobody experienced having an "eye put out" or was seriously injured, despite a lack of protective gear. Anybody who wore goggles or padding would've been laughed at.

There were always firecrackers. Solid fuel model rocket kits were popular at the time, but I took rocketry a step further into weaponry and rigged powerful firecrackers called M-80s to ignite when the rocket fuel was expended. Small rockets were cheap to build and thus disposable. My friend Keith, who would one day save my life, once shot a cow with a large, non-explosive model rocket. His expensive rocket was trashed, but the cow was unharmed.

In addition to minor crashes, I suffered my first major bicycle accident when I sped down a steep hill on my banana bike. I slammed into the driver's door of a parked car just as it swung open and went airborne. The driver yelled at me for screwing up his door. I was stunned and suffered major road rash, and my cherished bike was totaled.

As a good junior scientist, I read the classic book *Microbe Hunters* by Paul de Kruif, which inspired me to grow colorful and smelly fungal and bacterial forests. This probably didn't help my allergies. Annie caught me sterilizing my own piss in one of the household cooking pots, for use in a culture medium. After a "Lawd, Robert, what in sweet Jesus are you messin' with now!" I received a good whuppin'. The whuppin' is why this event stands out in my memory. Punishment, however, didn't dampen my fascination with living things.

My diet suffered after Charles died. While he was alive and healthy, the family had a substantial garden, a dairy cow, and chickens, plus we hunted and fished. For my first seven or eight years, I ate a good diet, if heavy in grease, as was most Southern cooking. Once Frances started working, processed food largely replaced her wholesome country cooking. We contributed to the decline of the Atlantic cod, eating boxes of frozen fish sticks. Lord knows what was in hot dogs and sausage back then. White bread, white rice, white pasta. Frozen vegetables boiled to tastelessness. Barely edible TV dinners. Pounds of sugar from soda, candy, and desserts. I was so skinny, I developed ulcers on my butt from sitting in hard school desk chairs. Things might've been different if I'd experienced a good diet and stable family life during my childhood and teen years. I might've grown inches taller and many pounds heavier in muscle, possessed better teeth, and been much smarter. I coulda been a contender.

I grew tall, regardless. I'm sure there were advantages, but it's been my experience that being at the ninety-eighth percentile for an American male's height (six-foot-three) is associated with health risks. I've lost count of the number of times I've hit my head on low-clearance obstacles. My scalp has significant scar tissue. My wife, Linda, tries to get me to wear a helmet at all times. I don't think I've ever suffered major concussions, or at least none I can remember, but I've come close. The world is engineered for the average, a uniformity of design contributing to my current neck and back issues. I suffer a stiff neck after parties and other social gatherings from bending over to converse with shorter folks.

Schools were integrated while I was in elementary school. The overtly racist George Wallace won a straw poll in my class before the 1968 presidential election. My aunt, neighbor, and grade-school teacher claimed, "Those little niggers just cain't learn." This was more a reflection of her lame teaching skills and racist attitudes than any inherent learning difficulties among students of color.

In Granite Quarry, riots didn't erupt after schools were integrated, but a lot of friction existed and plenty of fights broke out. For example, in junior high I saw four White high school football players beat the hell out of a Black friend my age who happened to be talking to a White girl. I started to intervene, but my friend warned me off and just took the beating. It's fortunate he wasn't severely injured.

I was never threatened by Black kids. However, I was threatened several times with beatings and torture, such as having my head dunked into a filthy toilet, by other White kids. The bullies included White racist kids with Klan parents who threatened me for my refusal to join them in talking shit, or worse, about Blacks. Klan begat Klan. I managed to avoid fights with them by taking an aggressive posture, balling my fists, and silently staring down my enemies. I suppose I received some mental reward from taking the moral high ground, or maybe I just didn't enjoy being fucked with, an attitude that persists to this day.

Yep, silent staring worked. They may have thought I was deranged, but after the first couple of times, I learned a valuable lesson. It's possible to intimidate yourself out of confrontation. Intimidation didn't always work, especially in fights with my brothers. It nearly always did outside the family, and served me well throughout life when dealing with male assholes. Avoiding fights was probably wise, as I have a bad temper. Allowing anger to take hold isn't the best defensive strategy. Early exposure to violent White racism on the part of local adults and my Klan Kid Klassmates also influenced my lifelong hatred of racism and bigotry in general. Bigotry is among the ugliest of human attributes.

⁂

Frances dated a lot of men. I didn't want to know why, although she was probably desperately lonely and sick of being a single mom. I don't recall the parade of men with clarity. Some might have been nice guys, but I found her behavior repulsive. I withdrew more in response to her becoming weirder due to her mental state and the crude drugs she was prescribed, but also to my siblings becoming wilder. I was active, but wasn't particularly athletic. I grew tall and looked emaciated by the time I was in junior high school. I was self-conscious and slumped. It took twenty years of yoga and physiotherapy to straighten myself out.

I found talking to girls difficult, despite having female friends in the neighborhood. I didn't understand that girls were just people. Frances thought I was odd for not having girlfriends and tried to set me up with daughters of friends, which made things worse.

I just wanted to escape my family, but I needed a door.

Ku Klux Klan march in Salisbury, North Carolina (1964). The young girl is perhaps only a few years older than me at the time (credit: archives of the University of North Carolina, Chapel Hill).

Charles Lee in his element, at one of his brother's property in western North Carolina (credit: F. Lee).

(above) I'm planning on creating some foul or toxic substance with my new chemistry set (credit: F. Lee).

(right) The sinister visage on this odd liddle feller is likely due to being a forced right-hander. I continued to bat right-handed even after I began to throw left-handed, for unclear reasons (credit: F. Lee).

The Mountain Door

I SOLO CLIMB A QUARTZITE ROCK ROUTE IN HANGING ROCK STATE PARK, ten stories off the deck. A light rain is falling. I have a death grip on the wet rock, and I'm forced to clean vegetation out of some of the cracks before I jam my bleeding fingers into them. My clumsy work boots don't help. They slip on the slimy rock. Watchful buzzards circle overhead, distinguished yet repellent, like soaring undertakers. They provide motivation for taking care while climbing, but I'm good at it. I attain a state of mental flow. I've never felt this alive, and the door to climbing opens wide.

⁂

When I was in junior high, Frances, my younger brother and I moved from our hometown of Granite Quarry to the larger town of Concord, North Carolina. The move was traumatic. Frances sought work and was dating a smelly, alcoholic, divorced Methodist minister who smoked. Bart rhymed with fart, so this is what we kids called him. I never understood what she saw in him, but she wasn't of stable mind. She was looking for love in all the wrong places. She started drinking more wine, which interacted with the prescription drugs she consumed. My older siblings had skedaddled by this point, so my younger brother and I were forced from a pleasant, rural home on an acreage, to a crappy little apartment in a crappy town and crappy new schools. This didn't help my introversion.

However, I discovered people did compelling and risky things in the mountains. I saw an ad in a magazine for an Outward Bound school featuring a dude *rapping* (rappelling, or sliding down a rope in a controlled fashion) down a cliff. Lo, it was in the North Carolina hills. The term rapping brings to mind the modern, energetic recitation of verse in an urban music context while hanging on a rope in the wilderness, but sadly, no. The Outward Bound ad suggested to me that risky mountain stuff was possible, and a school for it existed. I didn't realize risk isn't really what Outward Bound was or is about, but it piqued my interest. I lobbied my mother to go, but it cost too much, so my plan went nowhere. I saw a door worth climbing through, and resolved to take mountain adventure into my own hands.

I owned no proper clothing or gear, and the outdoor shops now peppering the physical and virtual landscapes didn't exist. In the South, if a young man was recreating outdoors and not hunting or fishing, he was viewed as somehow hinky, but I wanted more.

I lucked out, having neighbors in our apartment complex who went hiking and backpacking in the mountains as a standalone activity. They were a young, married, hippie couple from the Northeast, where this was more acceptable. They turned me on to the few mail order camping equipment firms at the time, which was a godsend. I just mailed a check for whatever I needed, and it was delivered via the magic of the US Postal Service. The catalogs were full of compelling photos of people doing cool things in the mountains and wilderness.

I had little money, so I ordered boots and camping gear, then hit the local Army-Navy surplus store for the rest. Good, specialized, outdoor clothing wasn't available anyway, and the surplus stuff was cheap. The Appalachians were cool and damp, so wool was advisable much of the year. I smelled like a moldy sheep while hiking, the unique Army-Navy store stink a pungent undertone.

Once I could drive, I borrowed Frances's car on weekends and headed for the hills. If I couldn't borrow her car, I'd hitchhike. All alone, in the ancient hardwood forests and eroded rock roots of a once great mountain range, I found self-reliance and sanity.

Frances suffered severe issues by then. For example, she screamed and beat the hell out of us with a large wooden rod when we acted up. I can still feel the accursed rod stinging my shoulders. I escaped whenever possible.

In addition to day-hiking in areas within a couple of hours' drive from home, I went backpacking on overnight trips in wilderness areas such as Great Smokies National Park. It rains a lot in the Appalachians, and my camping gear was marginal. I was often cold and wet, but I loved it. My solo Appalachian experiences provided a solid foundation for decades of working and recreating in the mountains.

I wasn't satisfied with hiking. I began to climb. I still had the Outward Bound rapping ad stuck in my head. I didn't know how to use a rope and had no money for gear, so I went without. I *soloed* (climbed without use of a rope) easy rock routes all over the Piedmont and southern Appalachians. Many of these areas are now crowded rock-climbing venues. Although I had no idea how to climb rock properly, I was naturally good at it. It didn't occur to me at the time, but sneakers might have made climbing easier than work or hiking boots. Sticky rubber-soled rock shoes had yet to be invented. I experienced one fall, but much later, so I must have been adept at managing climbing risk.

Why solo? I didn't know anybody else who was interested. This was the early 1970s, and I'm sure other climbers were out and about, but I never met or saw evidence of them. The Outward Bound school was near Linville Gorge, North Carolina, where I often hiked and climbed. According to Outward Bound's website, they climbed and rapped on Table Rock back then, but I never saw any Outward Bounders bounding outwards. I rarely saw anybody aside from tourists in parking lots.

The routes I soloed weren't difficult compared to today's standards, but I'm confident many were unclimbed, given I saw no signs of previous passage. It didn't occur to me to document or report the climbs, as is common practice in today's climbing world. I doubt a good mechanism existed for such reporting anyway, without the Internet. Nearly every major and minor cliff and hill in the world is now documented. I didn't document any of my climbs until much later, when I was laid up from a climbing accident. I never kept a journal. I just enjoyed climbing.

Psychologists study and describe a mental state called *flow*, in which a person is so focused on a physical or mental activity, nothing else matters. Time loses meaning. It's akin to a transcendent meditative state. The mental and emotional experience is so enjoyable, some people conduct the activity even at great risk and cost. Those who choose to do risky activities are often seeking the positive reward of the flow state. Risk focuses the mind like nothing else, in my experience. If it were possible, I'd be in a flow state on a continuous basis.

Solo climbing opened the door to flow states.

Most climbers use ropes and other equipment for safety on steep technical mountain, ice, and rock routes. A fall can be serious or fatal. To my knowledge, only a small percentage of climbers solo technical routes without a rope, but good statistics are lacking. Based on my reading, many people, even some climbers, think soloing is crazy and irresponsible.

I disagree. Soloing was, and still is, an important part of my life. It's difficult to explain the appeal of soloing to somebody who hasn't done it. There's a more intense connection between myself and the rock, ice, or mountain than when another person or persons are involved. Absent human-to-human communication, I feel like a highly focused animal flowing up the route. There are no distractions. A climber needs to be in a focused flow state to solo without dying. Additionally, soloing is much faster than roped climbing, so I could climb a route and return to safety quicker than if I used ropes.

Linda and I recently watched the excellent documentary *Free Solo*. The movie deserved and won an Academy Award, but it also caused much discussion in the non-climbing world about the sanity of its star. I don't know Alex Honnold, but he seems like one of the most rational contemporary climbers in his approach to risk management, as well as one of the world's greatest athletes. By rational, I mean dealing with dangerous situations using reasoned thought and action. After watching the film, I asked Linda what she thought of my soloing, and why she never objected to it.

She replied, "I knew you wouldn't do anything stupid, and I couldn't have stopped you anyway."

Not doing anything stupid is the key to not dying while soloing. There are climbers who solo climb far riskier routes than me, or even Honnold. They stay alive because they approach it rationally, unless they're just incredibly lucky.

One major misconception is that people who do risky stuff are adrenaline junkies or thrill seekers. As Honnold revealed in an interview, "If I get an adrenaline rush, something's gone wrong." I feel the same way. I don't want to experience thrills or adrenaline rushes at all while doing dangerous stuff, and neither does Linda, my usual climbing partner. I've experienced a few minor adrenaline rushes while climbing, but always in the context of incidents such as unexpectedly dislodging large rocks and nearly killing my wife below. I don't understand why anybody enjoys such rushes.

I don't view copious adrenaline release as an efficient or effective survival mechanism. Indeed, I consider it a strange outcome of evolution, or perhaps a holdover from prehistoric days. Staying calm is preferable. There could indeed be thrill seekers of many types who seek and enjoy adrenaline rushes, but I prefer rational risk management, which is addictive in itself. There's a sociology literature on *edgeworkers* or risk management addicts exploring how different types of risk-seeking people and groups view and manage risk.

There was risk associated with running into backwoods denizens living in the hills, back in the day. The John Boorman movie *Deliverance* wasn't exaggerated, but I managed to avoid any porcine-like encounters. However, I've had firearms pointed at me. The first was a shotgun in the hands of a hillbilly as I hiked past his tarpaper shack near the Appalachian Trail. He admonished, "Git off my property." Even though I wasn't on his property, I picked up my pace and git.

The next occasion involved a rifle in the hands of a whiskey-breathed hunter. I made the mistake of hiking in what would one day be designated the Joyce Kilmer-Slickrock Wilderness Area, early the first morning of black bear season. I came around a bend in the trail, and the drunk hunter swung around, literally loaded for bear. Looking down the large-caliber barrel from the wrong end, I put up my hands in a cowboy surrender and he lowered his weapon. As I no longer hunted, I resolved to avoid gun hunting season after this encounter.

In the early 1970s, our family moved to the small college town of Chapel Hill, North Carolina. Shortly after, Frances married Bart. They and my younger brother moved temporarily to Charlotte, where Bart worked. Frances and Bart decided I would stay in Chapel Hill. The logic of all this was unclear, and I don't recall having a say in the decision.

Regardless, I lived alone in Bart's ancient travel trailer, stinking of booze and cigarette smoke, parked in a seedy trailer park. Yep, I was teen trailer-trash, thrown alone into a town and school about as different from Granite Quarry or Concord as can be imagined, and still be in the South. Chapel Hill called itself a "pat of butter in a sea of grits," as its population was and probably still is better educated, wealthier, and more liberal than surrounding areas. It was a shock to a kid from Klansville.

I didn't have a car and couldn't afford one, but needed one to get to high school from the trailer park. Bart left me with a beat up 1950s panel truck. He wasn't all bad. I drove it to the mountains and boondocked in it. I even bought chains for it so I could escape in the winter.

For a normal high-school boy, having his own trailer and ride might have been a sweet deal with regard to partying and the ladies, although the trailer and ride were far from cool. I was also terribly introverted, a condition exacerbated by Frances and Bart's toxic relationship and our frequent moves.

I still suffered from the early nerd-branding. I'd developed bad acne and had no money for fashionable clothes. I tried to grow a beard to cover up my acne, which made me look even more like a hayseed. Frances gave me dorky haircuts, and I wore thick, black-framed nerd-glasses. I didn't drink or do drugs. My diet consisted largely of hot dogs and hamburgers I cooked in the Stink-Trailer. I don't recall eating any vegetables. I was six-foot-three, and only weighed one-hundred-sixty pounds. I was never invited to parties.

There's sketchy evidence, or perhaps it's a myth, that some women find men who engage in risky activities to be more attractive. It didn't apply in my case. I was surprised later when I read about and met climbers who claimed many women wanted to be with them, as the women found risk-takers attractive. Maybe they were better climbers or better looking than me, or maybe I didn't advertise enough. Or perhaps, I just didn't meet any girls or women who suffered this weird affliction. I never had a date in high school, and never kissed or even held a girl's hand.

Although I suffered socially in high school, I was somewhat fit despite my awful diet. I could run in long-distance track and cross-country competitions, but not well. I tried playing basketball, but I was so skinny I just got knocked about in the bumper-car game under the basket. I played woodwinds in the concert and marching bands, but not well. I preferred the drums, but there were too many other budding drummers who were better than me.

I scored a job on a grounds crew at the University of North Carolina (UNC) with several older stoners. They were nice guys and fun to work with. I just didn't get the stoner part. The work provided money for gas and outdoor gear. Apart from the routine risks experienced outdoors in North Carolina, such as heat, poison ivy, and hornets, the job resulted in a crushed fingertip while loading a large boulder onto a truck. The guy I was helping lost his grip, and my finger found itself between a rock and a hard place. I now have eleven fingernails. When the finger healed, the nail grew out double, but this is preferable to a missing finger.

I went to the mountains for entertainment. I also discovered science fiction around this time, which resulted in my becoming a voracious reader of this genre. I don't recall ever being depressed; I always had my mountains and books. I'm unsure how I would've manifested depression anyway. I was terribly lonely with regard to girls, but I couldn't see a way out of my situation.

Chapel Hill High School had an excellent academic reputation, being in a college town. I discovered I could take college credit courses. However, Frances declared the only way I could go to college was to win a scholarship, because she had no money. I wasn't good enough in athletics, but I was good enough in academics, at least for an in-state tuition. I saw an eventual escape from my mother's sphere, although not an escape from the South.

As expected, Frances divorced Bart. She and my younger brother moved back to Chapel Hill, and I escaped trailer-trash-dom. I now had access to my mother's cars. She tended to buy cars equipped with powerful V-8 engines, even though she didn't have a need and wasn't a confident driver. Her driving skills were marginal at best, but worsened because she was stoned on sedatives, antidepressants, anxiolytics, wine, and god knows what else, on a continuous basis. Being a passenger with her at the wheel was rather tense at times.

I enjoyed her attraction to these cars, as long as she wasn't driving. They weren't so-called muscle cars, but they were powered by muscular engines. Once I discovered driving fast was entertaining, I borrowed Frances's car and went flying down the twisty back roads. It was akin to driving a boat at a hundred miles per hour in choppy water without being able to see what was ahead, and unreliable handling if quick reaction was necessary. Her boat-ish cars weren't equipped with stiff suspensions like the true muscle cars of the day; they were even riskier than those muscular pieces of shit. Fortunately, I've been blessed with fast reaction time.

Driving fast and well required extreme focus, which became a rewarding and important part of my life. Climbing also requires extreme focus. Driving to the mountains allowed me to both drive fast and recreate in the hills, resulting in added reward and also cumulative risk of injury or death. I may have been less risk-averse back then.

Driving through this door may not have been prudent, but at least it resulted in a good set of vehicular risk management skills.

Frances began working for Don, a physician faculty member at UNC. I did some yard work for him, and discovered he and a physician buddy went fishing every year in a fantastical land called the Wind River Range in Wyoming. I'd never been out of the South. I didn't have a particular interest in fishing, although Wyoming's Green River was world-class at the time. The foot-long trout practically leaped into your arms. I was more interested in backpacking. I was tired of hiking in the Appalachian woods, rarely even enjoying a view. I convinced Frances to let me join Don the following summer. She agreed, most likely glad to get rid of the kids however she could.

Don kindly gave me a copy of *The Complete Walker* by the pioneering Colin Fletcher. This was the first backpacking instructional book. It was also packed with tales of the author's wild adventures, such as the first continuous foot trek down the Grand Canyon. Fletcher's practice of hiking alone resonated with me, if not his tendency to hike naked whenever he could.

I drove to the Wind Rivers with Don and his friend in a VW microbus. I enjoyed interacting with two intelligent adults who treated me well. They thought I was amusing, which may or may not have been intentional. My first sight of the Front Range of the Rockies, after suffering through the Great Plains, is burned in my memory. I can retrieve the image even now.

Once we arrived, they car-camped and fished. I took off on two, week-long solo backpacks, mostly in trailless terrain. I saw nobody. I fished for my breakfasts and dinners. The Wind Rivers are grizzly and wolf country, but I had no close encounters. I was prepared to a reasonable degree, and I think Don had faith I wouldn't do anything stupid. I even took my first ice ax, which I still have. I encountered my first permanent snowfields. I was gobsmacked by the alpine vistas. The trip instantly hooked me on real mountains, as opposed to the worn down Appalachian stumps.

I strode through the Western mountain door.

My looming Vietnam draft registration was a major inflection point in high school. Yep, high school. Shipping off to a foreign country and being shot at while trudging through fetid tropical swamps felt like something to avoid, although many boys didn't have a choice. In the interest of risk management, I'd been thinking ahead.

Frances knew a North Carolina Congressman through her job. We discussed the possibility of applying for the Air Force Academy. A recommendation from a member of Congress was essential to getting accepted. Flying seemed a preferable alternative to swamp trudging. I would've found the physical requirements difficult, as I was so skinny, but bullet-ridden-swamp avoidance was a powerful motivator. Applying to the Air Force Academy was unnecessary, however. Richard Nixon stopped the Vietnam draft in 1973. I dodged a lot of literal bullets by chance policy timing.

I would've enjoyed flying, but despite my family's long military history, I had and still have strong moral objections to killing for any reason. Being drafted or joining up and going to Vietnam probably wasn't a good plan for a pacifist. Aside from the moral objections, I don't react well to people ordering me around, a lifelong personality trait affecting my work and educational choices. It was fortunate I avoided the military. I probably would've ended up court-martialed.

As for working in conflict zones, hospital emergency rooms (ERs), as a first responder, or other dangerous jobs, I respect such folks, but I was never interested or committed enough to seek such a career. Like most people, my aversion or tolerance to particular types of risk is complex. I was also always aware of cumulative risk.

By the time I graduated high school, my family had disintegrated. I no longer cared. I just wanted to be on my own. I won an academic scholarship to North Carolina State University (State), and relief was in sight.

The parents of a popular kid hosted a large high school graduation party, and everybody was invited. I attended my first teen party. Many adults were invited as well. This was a shock to my world view. The parents were wealthy, hippie, university professors, living in what would now be a large multi-million-dollar house in Chapel Hill. I'd never been in such a home.

Partiers were met at the door by the parents, who charged admission. The rate depended on whether partiers were drinking, smoking weed (cannabis), or taking psychedelic drugs such as psilocybin mushrooms and lysergic acid diethylamide (LSD). The parents had purchased alcohol and drugs for the teenagers, which I expect wasn't common or remotely appropriate, even back in hippie days.

I haven't attended a party quite like it since, and I've partied hearty over the years. I'd previously tried sips of piss-water American beer and found it vile. I observed everybody else having a high old time, so I choked down two or three. I found the alcohol buzz interesting, but not compelling. Rather, I found the entire scene weird and overwhelming. The house was clouded with weed smoke. Psychedelically dilated pupils were the norm. Both students and adults appeared to be making out, or more, in the back rooms. Aside from beer, I didn't try any of the drugs, didn't interact much, had no sex, and left alone. Those doors remained closed until I entered State's doors.

The Perception Door

The fall trees are blazing. I ride my bike to an area of old forest near Raleigh. The psychedelic drug I've ingested takes at least an hour to take effect. By the time I hike down to a stream, I'm blazing, along with the trees. I have difficulty walking because of the extreme detail I see in the foliage and leaf litter. Luminescent colors glow and shimmer. I sit on a flat rock in the middle of the stream. I'm rooted there for five or six hours, although I feel no sense of time passing, apart from observing the position of the sun. I'm completely dissociated from my body. The water flows around and through me, and I'm immersed in the ultimate manifestation of a flow state. I hear ants walking. Eyes closed, I can still see. I feel serene, tranquil, and at peace; interconnected with the natural world. I trip into the next day. The door to true perception opens wide, and I experience Blake's Infinity.

I was accepted to North Carolina State's Forestry program, and a set of life-changing doors manifested themselves. I wanted to be a forest ranger but had romantic notions of what it meant. Forestry typically involves killing trees, which I gathered a little late in the game. I loved living trees and lost interest.

I still found plants and other life to be fascinating, so I switched to Botany. It would've been difficult to choose a more useless science major in terms of gainful employment, but I wasn't thinking clearly about a career. Botany provided a good foundation in biology, however, which is essential to understanding the wonders of life. I'd been captivated by the natural world since my free-range youth in the diverse ecology of the inland South.

Coincidentally, several friends from Granite Quarry attended State at the same time. We did good ol' boy things together, playing basketball, rocking to tunes, playing cards, drinking beer (which had become more tolerable by this time), and talking about women (all talk, in my case). I discovered I could throw a frisbee well, which sounds like a minor skill, but I was willing to embrace anything allowing me to fit in. I slowly found a social circle.

I went back home to Chapel Hill as little as possible.

State had an outdoor club. The members were all male, as outdoors stuff wasn't as popular with females in those days. Additionally, State's student body was ninety percent men at the time, so the lack of women wasn't surprising. I wasn't interested in most of the activities, but I heard a few of the guys were planning a trip out West. Yee-haw! The wrinkle was, they wanted to attempt the first winter ascents of some peaks in Rocky Mountain National Park in Colorado over Christmas break. They were all Yankees and claimed they'd done winter mountaineering in New England. They seemed to know what they were doing. I owned an ice ax, so what the hell.

The four of us geared up and embarked in a tiny station wagon. I forgot the names of the destination peaks for many years. A winter technical climb on Mt. Lady Washington decades later jogged my memory. We planned to climb other peaks as well, but this was the only one we summited, via the easiest route. How my partners knew this peak hadn't been climbed in winter wasn't clear, and I've been unable to verify whether this was indeed the case.

The difficulty of the expedition was a little over our heads. None of us were strong or fit enough. I strained under my cheap backpack, which weighed over sixty pounds. We were excruciatingly slow, and suffered continuous cold in our inadequate woolen clothing. Good synthetic clothing and insulation hadn't been invented yet.

It snowed the entire time. Avalanches slithered and crashed all around us, and it was below zero Fahrenheit at night. The brutal wind ripped the stitches of our cheap mountain tents. At least we had the foresight to pack large shovels, so we built a snow cave, and nestled in the snow wells of large boulders. We also carried gallons of gasoline fuel, which is one reason the packs were so heavy, but at least we could eat and drink lots of hot stuff.

We smelled like foul damp sheep in our woolens. Waterproof-but-breathable fabric shell sleeping bags didn't yet exist. We tried to stay warm in goose down bags that accumulated body and external moisture, especially in the snow cave. They grew damp, then sodden—useless by the end of the week-long trip. We wore non-insulated leather boots and an early form of *super-gaiters* (insulated sleeves covering the entire boot except the sole), which didn't work well. Several of my toes were numb for years afterwards. At least I didn't lose any.

There was so much fresh powder, we post-holed up to our knees even with snowshoes, and struggled to the corniced summit of the only peak we climbed. It was amazing we didn't start avalanches or get avalanched upon. None of us knew anything about the science of snow stability.

We never got a view of anything. Not the best introduction to winter mountaineering, but at least we all kept our shit together. I never heard about any similar trips again, and I lost interest in the club's activities due to other, emerging interests. I also never related to the other guys. We had little in common, and I was still introverted.

However, I'd opened a crack in the winter mountaineering door.

I tried to fit in otherwise at State, but it didn't go well, at least in the beginning. For example, disco was at its peak. I went to a few dances and stood around nursing piss-water beers. I just didn't understand the alien disco scene. Actual dancing, which I'd never done, was an essential part of disco, as were ridiculous clothes, and copious amounts of alcohol, cocaine, and sex. It was probably fun, but it wasn't my bag. I got stinking drunk once. Puking beer was so revolting I didn't care to repeat the experience. Observing drunk people do stupid things contributed to my aversion.

And I didn't like disco music. I was much more into 1960s and 1970s psychedelic and progressive stoner music, although I wasn't yet a stoner. This type of music had spoken to me since the Granite Quarry days. I rocked to artists such as Hendrix, Santana, Cream, and Zeppelin, crackling from my tiny transistor radio late at night.

A campus housing shortage existed when I first arrived, and I couldn't afford off-campus housing. I was initially placed in temporary housing in a gym with cots, and later crammed into a two-person dorm room with two other guys.

Dorms were perilous places. There were frequent fights, but I managed to avoid pissing others off. I learned to peek into the hallway before exiting the room to avoid suffering near-beheading by a frisbee or football thrown down the hall. Communal bathrooms often attracted assholes. Unseen bombers waited until I was taking a shit, feet bound by my pants, to throw in a handful of firecrackers and slam the door. Unseen tossers tossed ice cold water on my crotch while I was washing my hair in the shower.

After several months of residential misery, a room in the athletes' dorm opened up with a single roommate. This was a relief. The dorms were newer and the rooms were much larger and nicer than the dismal warrens of the nonathlete dorms. This dorm housed a mix of male athletes and nonathletes; everyone partied hearty.

I tapped on the door of my assigned room, which was locked and bolted. After a surly, "Who the hell is it?" and some rustling, my new roommate, Randy, opened the door. He'd been busy cleaning and bagging ten pounds— yes, pounds—of high-grade, Jamaican cannabis, which he'd hidden under his bed on a bedsheet.

I was shocked but rolled with it. I'd seen and smelled stoners smoking weed in high school and my UNC job, but smoking in general seemed unhealthy to me, so I never partook. I'm also not sure I could've handled my family in a stoned state.

Randy was not only a stoner, he made a tidy sum selling weed and occasionally, other drugs. He was tall, handsome, funny, knew how to work the discos, and had lots of drugs; so, he also had sex with an impressive number of women.

After a few weeks, I tried smoking weed, but I experienced no effects aside from coughing my lungs out. It wasn't because of low potency. A common misconception is cannabis is much stronger now, compared to the past. Perhaps this is true on average, but it wasn't the case in the Raleigh area. The three universities in the Raleigh, Chapel Hill, and Durham area comprised an enormous market for drugs, and they were on a major south-north importation pipeline from Florida to the Northeast. I had access to the finest, including high-test hashish, which is packed with the psychoactive chemical tetrahydrocannabinol (THC). My gristly brain simply wouldn't accept a buzz.

One semester, Randy was at risk of flunking out from partying way too hearty. He stopped smoking weed, handed me a bong and his last ounce of fine Columbian bud, and told me to have at it. Despite daily bong hits, still nada. But a few weeks later, I felt my first buzz. I stayed high for the next ten years, except when in class, studying, or working.

I floated through a life-changing pharmaceutical door.

I found the rewards associated with most illegal drugs I inhaled or consumed to be substantial, but I could manage the substantial risks. Back in the day, the stoner term for pharmaceutical risk management was *maintaining*. In all of my drug experiences, with one major exception, I was able to maintain just fine. Those experiences were transformative.

Many people consider recreational drug use a moral failure of some sort. Some refer to escapism, as if you are trying to escape your own brain. Yet many of those same people drink alcohol or take mind-altering prescription drugs, or for that matter engage in practices as diverse as sex and prayer, all with potent cognitive effects. I believe everybody should have the freedom to choose their own path in changing their brain chemistry, as long as they don't harm others. However, *in no way* do I suggest or recommend anybody take the particular path I followed.

It's surprising I graduated, much less kept my scholarship. The point of a university education is to learn something, although I don't recall learning much I didn't already know. I learned to balance my time between being high, working, and studying. Working and studying while stoned weren't enjoyable, so I didn't. There was a significant social aspect to drug use, which I greedily consumed after my pathetic and lonely high school period. I now enjoyed a large and diverse circle of friends.

My alcohol use was moderate after my disco puking episode. *Downers* (for example, Quaaludes), and *uppers* (speed, or amphetamines) didn't interest me. Downers made me sluggish and brain-dead, similar to diphenhydramine, and uppers made me twitchy and aggro. Opiates were limited, but these weren't of great interest. Cocaine might have been of interest, but it was too expensive for me, and thus I was limited to snorting it when wealthier friends shared.

I attended State from 1975 to 1979, so I missed the peak of the hippie era. Vietnam was over, and the Age of Aquarius was obviously not happening. State wasn't exactly a hotbed of the so-called counterculture. It was an engineering and agricultural university as opposed to a liberal arts school. I knew a few hippies, wealthy Yankees who somehow ended up at State, but I never felt part of their tribe.

There were aspects of the hippie tribe I adopted, such as drugs and long hair; but I never saw the appeal of the Grateful Dead, dreads, flowing ethnic clothing, and patchouli. I also had to work, which few hippies appeared to do. I would've welcomed free love with open, naked arms, but this didn't happen to me. I didn't belong to the hippie, disco, or athlete tribes, who seemed to bogart all the sex.

The balance between studies and non-studies became more challenging when I encountered psychedelic drugs. Required reading for stoners at the time was Aldous Huxley's *The Doors of Perception*. I found the book fascinating. I didn't find Carlos Castaneda's mythological stuff as interesting. Ken Kesey's and Timothy Leary's adventures just seemed wacko to me.

I wasn't seeking spiritual enlightenment or a higher plane of being. I sought novel experience and freedom of thought. Unlike Huxley, the first ten or so times I took psychedelic drugs I only experienced slightly heightened visual awareness, despite large doses. A whopping dose of LSD at a Jethro Tull concert cured this. The band morphed into a troupe of harlequins, and the music permeated my brain.

I saw the far side of the psychedelic door, and it was a revelation.

I consumed psilocybin mushrooms or 'shrooms, LSD, refined or synthetic mescaline and psilocybin, and more; well over one hundred trips through the door over a period of years. I never truly hallucinated, or saw nonexistent things while my eyes were open, although I came close.

I befriended a high-level dealer through Randy, and I gained access to a higher drug plane. Walter was a most unlikely drug dealer in appearance, which he cultivated to a careful degree. He was short, stocky, and had short hair combed to the side in an era of ubiquitous long hippie hair. He wore nerdy clothing and thick, black-framed glasses in an era of wireframes. He even wore a calculator on his belt. In other words, he had the attributes of a bona fide nerd, a shorter version of me in high school. However, he lived in a continuously stoned state and was a high-level dealer on campus. He liked me because we shared an interest in good music and science fiction, and I could maintain. We could carry on an intelligent conversation while taking quantities of drugs that would cause most people to cringe in a closet until they came down.

I never bought from Walter; indeed, he wouldn't have sold to me. His drug buddy circle of trust was four or five people. A couple were chemistry graduate students. If he acquired something interesting, he'd call me up and say, "Come on over," with no further explanation. He expected me to arrive, no matter the time of day, whether I had an upcoming exam or other commitment. If I failed to appear, I'd miss a golden pharmaceutical opportunity.

I had access to a wide variety of high-quality products, including the only uncut cocaine I ever snorted, which made me feel like a superior form of being. We marveled at the first killer Hawaiian bud he obtained. He once scored some pharmaceutical-grade THC. After smoking this, I walked back to my dorm and couldn't feel the ground beneath my feet. Walter was also the doorman to high-quality psychedelics.

Risks associated with psychedelics involved obtaining the actual drug being represented (as opposed to another chemical), quality and age of the drug, and dosing. Predicting cognitive changes, and thus being able to maintain while tripping, were critical. Tripping out could be deadly if the tripper couldn't maintain, especially if he was doing something dangerous like rock climbing. A much leaner and largely word-of-mouth body of information existed back then about drugs, compared to the copious amount of information now available in books and on the Internet.

Relating to other people while tripping could be challenging. With low doses of LSD or milder psychedelics such as 'shrooms, interacting with people in social settings was a blast. With high doses of LSD or other potent psychedelics, I found the trips were more enjoyable and rewarding when I was alone outside in natural surroundings. I couldn't imagine tripping my brains out in the muddy crowd at Woodstock, for example. Perhaps one had to be a hippie.

There was and probably still is a great deal of blind trust in obtaining the actual drug and dose being proffered. This was particularly important with synthetic drugs, as they often came in the form of a nondescript white powder or pill. Obtaining drugs from a familiar dealer or friend whom I trusted and who'd consumed it themselves was important. This was an early and personal realization of the toxicological maxim of Paracelsus, "The dose makes the poison." This maxim was particularly important with psychedelics, the dosages in micrograms and the duration of effect many hours. Knowing Walter was therefore a great advantage.

One spring, he obtained hundreds of doses of pure LSD, administered in sugar cubes. Each cube contained 500 micrograms, a substantial dose. He didn't want to keep such a large quantity in his dorm room. As opposed to *blotter* LSD dried on tiny squares of paper, the sugar cubes presented storage problems, so he asked me if I'd keep some for him in a dorm refrigerator. The risk of storing the dosed sugar was balanced by the fact that I could consume as much as I wanted, with the understanding I wouldn't sell any.

Additionally, a limited number of jumbo-sized sugar cubes were included as a bonus, dosed with STP or Serenity, Tranquility, and Peace. STP is 2, 5-dimethoxy-4-methylamphetamine, also called DOM. It's a psychedelic as opposed to a speedy form of amphetamine, a sort of super-LSD in terms of effect and duration. Given a large dose, most people trip more than twenty-four hours.

I worked full-time in the summers and didn't need to worry about my studies, but I still stayed on campus; I certainly didn't want to go home. So, for about three months, I took a sugar cube almost every weekend. I also tripped during the school year, if I didn't have an upcoming exam. These trips included three STP experiences during the spectacular autumn foliage season.

These trips blew the doors of perception wide open. It's difficult to describe such trips in a way those who haven't taken such drugs would understand. Each person's journey is unique. The religious may "see a god," I suppose. I wasn't and thus didn't, but I experienced universal connectedness. There's no greater joy. Decades later, I can still recall many trips with clarity.

On high-dose LSD and STP trips, no distinction between myself and the environment existed. It wasn't hallucination; it was dissolution of self. There was no meaning, only being, a peek through one of many doors to cognitive enlightenment.

Some people are frightened by the prospect of integration into the environment and loss of self. Fear is commonly defined as a strong primal emotion induced by perceived danger. Fear causes physiological changes and behavioral changes such as fleeing, hiding, or freezing. These effects have never happened to me. I don't know why. Perhaps my lack of fear response is partially genetic. I can't imagine my father was afraid of anything at all. My lack of fear response may explain much of my risky life, but there are lots of people who repeatedly engage in risky activities, despite their fear.

Waking up the next morning, still tripping, was a surprise the first time I took STP. After multiple trips, I began to feel some apprehension I'd get stuck in a tripping state. It was unlikely, but the possibility of an extended duration spent in a massively altered state was a bit much.

Those who practice meditation can sometimes attain similar states, but this requires decades of extensive study and practice in a controlled environment. It ain't something you can just pick up in a weekly yoga class. I was far from ready for this level of rigorous commitment. The third STP trip was the last time I took powerful, multi-day psychedelics. Not so, for low-dose LSD and shorter-duration psychedelics, which I continued to take for years. Much later, I made one exception to the no-multi-day trip rule.

I conducted a number of risky activities while tripping. For example, I liked to drive fast while tripping on mild psychedelics such as 'shrooms, and high on weed. These drugs didn't affect my coordination and reaction times. No alcohol though, as driving drunk is just stupid.

I bought a rode-hard-and-put-away-wet 1965 Mustang before leaving for State. It had its issues, but it still galloped to a hundred. I drove the faster cars of friends, with their permission, including a GTO, Camaro SS, Chevelle SS, Charger Superbee, and the like. I topped out the speedometers of these V-8 powered beasts on brief North Carolina backroad straights. There were more straight sections of road east of Raleigh compared to the Piedmont and in the mountains. Fortunately, most of these cars handled better than the boat-ish cars Frances owned.

I drove fast often, never had an accident, never got a ticket, and never lost control, a state I've never quite understood. It brings to mind a driver throwing his hands up and shouting, "Jesus, take the wheel!" However, a seminal event occurred while tripping on 'shrooms, alone behind the wheel of the Superbee, cruising over a hundred miles per hour. The machine's four-forty with a six-pack of carb barrels was screaming like a giant lawn-mower. The trees blurred. I focused on staying on the pavement, as any distraction could've been deadly. I achieved flow in the high-speed moment. But I suddenly realized driving such a powerful vehicle this fast outside of a track or closed course crossed a risky red line. The rewards weren't sufficient to justify the potential loss, including my life. This was a spontaneous and personal invocation of decision analysis, which evaluates tradeoffs between loss and reward.

I pulled over, sat for a while, smoked some weed, and listened to some tunes. I drove home at the posted speed limit, and never drove that fast again unless it was on a racetrack. I also never drove again under the influence of psychedelic drugs.

I explored State's campus and nearby abandoned buildings at night while tripping, sometimes with buddies, and sometimes alone. I could see better at night in this state. I don't know whether improved night vision is common to psychedelic drug use, but it makes physiological sense. Pupil dilation, common in people who take psychedelics, may allow more light to enter the eye.

I owned a pellet air rifle with a large flashlight taped to the barrel, which I toted on my nighttime excursions to manage rat risk in old buildings. I never shot any rats, but they were plentiful. Flocks of roosting pigeons would burst into noisy flight when disturbed. Herds of cockroaches and other unpleasant insect life skittered around my feet. Rotten floorboards and stair treads required a light step. Such horror movie settings sometimes failed to enhance the psychedelic drug experiences of my companions. Some freaked out and never joined me again.

And there was always climbing on psychedelics. I could've tried to find partners, but the guys on the Colorado trip, for example, didn't impress me with their wilderness knowledge and skills. I preferred going alone at the time, anyway. Since I couldn't afford to go anywhere else, I stayed in the southern Appalachians.

I continued to solo rock climb, while tripping on 'shrooms or refined psilocybin, along with smoking weed. I was completely at ease hiking and climbing while stoned and mildly tripping. The psilocybin high didn't last as long as LSD, and I stayed out until I came down. Sometimes I camped and went home the next day. I never saw anybody else climbing. Climbing still wasn't popular in the Southeast, although according to my Colorado climbing partners it was popular in the Northeast.

Climbing while tripping was transcendent. The lichens and vegetation on the rock vibrated with heightened color and life. I felt a synergy between the focused act of climbing and my psychedelically altered state, reached states of flow, and experienced great personal gratification. This is difficult to explain to those who are not, as Jimi Hendrix once described, "experienced." A crude description might be, being one with the rock. However, it went far beyond.

Climbing, skiing, surfing, and other dangerous activities while stoned and tripping don't appear to be unusual, based on my subsequent research and conversations with outdoor athletes. However, this is rarely discussed outside the respective adventure tribes. Many nonathletes consider these risky activities to be crazy enough in a non-drugged state. They certainly wouldn't understand the appeal of undertaking such dangerous pursuits while tripping on mind-altering drugs.

❧

During one of my climbs, a handhold broke free. I fell about ten feet onto a ledge, gashing my right leg in the process. I bandaged the wound, down-climbed, hiked to the car, cleaned the gash and bandaged it again, and drove home. I learned a valuable lesson, the scars on my right leg as a vivid reminder. Always test your hand and footholds. However, the fall did nothing to stop me from climbing while tripping and stoned. Climbing was the high point of my life.

Many rock climbers consider it normal to fall if they use a rope and clip it to solid *pro* (protection) lodged in solid rock. Rock pro may be aluminum nuts, spring-loaded camming devices (cams), or pitons. Expansion bolts are permanent pro, placed in holes drilled into the rock. Modern sport climbers on bolted routes climb at their limits to advance their skills, which means they may routinely fall off, protected by the rope clipped to pro. This applies to climbing in a gym as well.

In contrast, I find the practice of routine falling to be strange, as it assumes a level of trust in equipment and your own body I've never had. Even if a climber is roped, has good pro, and the route is steep; if they fall, they can still swing and slam into the rock, risking injury.

Later in life, I lamented to my partner Linda that I hadn't started climbing difficult roped routes until my thirties. I wondered what I would've been like if I'd started technical climbing as a teenager or younger and pushed my limits more.

Her reply: "Well, you'd either be very good, or you'd be dead."

A rich mountaineering literature didn't exist in the 1970s. The limited number of books in local libraries consisted of expedition accounts that were either clinical and boring, or nauseating in their jingoistic fervor and self-congratulation. Expedition climbing seemed so far removed from rock climbing, I couldn't imagine myself in those situations. It sounded like misery to me, especially considering my Colorado experience. The concept of using ropes just seemed like a lot of work.

I read a book about John Gill, a pioneer in *bouldering* (un-roped, difficult rock climbing requiring gymnastic skill). His athleticism was so far above mine I just couldn't relate. I also couldn't relate to attempting hard routes over and over again, which is what many boulderers enjoy. It sounded boring to me.

Many climbers I've talked to over the years spoke of inspiring climbing books, read in their youth. Not me. Writers such as John Muir and Aldo Leopold inspired me to hike and explore the wilderness, but I can't think of any early mountaineering literature I read that conveyed the love of experiences in wild places I felt and sought. So, I just did what I liked.

I also didn't consider it a big deal, in the greater scheme of things, to climb a cliff or mountain, no matter how big or difficult it was. I still don't. Climbing is a pointless activity to everyone except the climbers themselves. I found it especially ridiculous that "conquering" a mountain could be viewed as some sort of nationalistic achievement. A lasting peace with your neighbors is an accomplishment, not some homeboys hacking their way up a giant hunk of rock and ice. Nobody "conquers" mountains, regardless. Mountains allow people to climb them.

A similar experience to solo climbing occurred while I was tripping on 'shrooms and hiking through the woods near Raleigh. I spied a log spanning a narrow and rocky dry gully. The log was maybe twenty feet long, narrowing from about sixteen to eight inches in diameter, ten feet above the bottom of the gully. I decided to walk across.

The log started out solid but became more and more flexible as I approached the narrow end. With every step, the log flexed and shook, but it was difficult to retreat. A fall meant a sprain or break. Hitting my head on the rocks at the bottom could have killed me. So, I took a couple of deep breaths, waited for the log to stop vibrating, focused, and walked across calmly and carefully. I sat for some time on the far side pondering this experience.

Like solo climbing, this woody slack-line experience involved stepping through a critical door that required staying focused, maintaining in a risky situation, and simply getting through it. In contrast, I could slow down or stop when driving a car fast. A flow state in a dynamic risk situation with no escape can be highly rewarding, but sometimes I wanted to get it over with as soon as possible so I could live another day.

Another set of wild trips involved water. The North and South Carolina coastal plain of marshes and swamps is a primordial landscape seething with life. The cypress swamps are trippy *sans* psychedelics, and alien worlds *avec*; black water and ancient trees festooned with the epiphytic Spanish Moss. Swimming in the ocean while tripping was otherworldly. The North Carolina coast at the time was sparsely populated, and I could walk miles of beach with nobody else around. The sand was peppered with interesting, beautiful, and often pungent live and dead marine life.

I was never a good swimmer. Due to my density and low body fat, I tend to sink in fresh water, but I can float in the sea. Despite a few sketchy moments in the ocean with The Under Toad and Portuguese Men-of-War, these visits were highly enjoyable experiences. I'd stay in the water for hours and get pruney. It's amazing I didn't get fried from sunburn.

One sketchy fresh water event was at a local quarry. North Carolina, including the town of Granite Quarry, is dotted with old, hard-rock quarries. When depleted or when they go out of business, they often fill with water. Vertical walls allow dives off the edge in relative safety.

Keith, my childhood friend from Granite Quarry who shot the cow with a rocket, was an excellent swimmer and lifeguard. He and I visited one of these quarries near Chapel Hill on a spring day. I was tripping on a healthy dose of LSD, and we had both been smoking weed. We dove off a thirty-foot cliff. On the first dive I hit the water with great force, descended through steadily colder water, and saw a bunch of trash and large machinery on the bottom. I looked up and realized the surface was far above me. This was disconcerting, but manageable.

Cliff-diving was entertaining, but then Keith expressed the desire to swim across the quarter-mile wide quarry. I had misgivings, as I wasn't a good swimmer in fresh water.

Keith suggested, "Just backstroke if you get tired."

Halfway across, my legs began to cramp. I remember looking up at the sky and calmly preparing to drown. But it quickly occurred to me Keith wasn't far away. I motioned and called for him.

He hauled ass over to me, assisted me to shore, and asked if I wanted to leave.

"No, let's dive off the cliff a few more times first," I said. I had to jump back on that watery horse, but learned a lesson about my swimming limits.

Sadly, Keith, the only person besides Linda to ever directly save my life, killed himself after college. I never learned why.

$\sim$

My roommate Randy and I took a skydiving lesson at a rural airport in eastern North Carolina during this period. The training was rudimentary at best. Something along the lines of, "Okay, now y'all jump out the plane."

It was hellishly hot, the instructors sketchy ex-military rednecks, the equipment smelly military surplus, and the plane rickety. When the time came to steer the big dome-shaped chutes, the jumpers were to look down and aim in the direction indicated by a dude on the ground manning a big white plywood arrow on a pivot. Steering the huge dome was more difficult than steering a modern parachute or parasail rig. We were also told to avoid landing in a particular farmer's field. If we were to do so, he'd run out with a shotgun and hold us there until somebody picked us up.

The single-engine airplane rattled as if it were self-destructing. When the time came to jump, I stepped out on the plane's wheel as instructed, gripping the angled wing strut. I was blasted by an eighty mile per hour wind. Instead of stepping back and assuming the stable aerodynamic skydiver position I'd been shown, I made the mistake of just letting go of the wing strut. I backflipped several times before the static line pulled my chute. My puke likely pelted onlookers. At least I didn't land in Shotgun Farmer's field.

I found this experience highly unpleasant, got no jollies from it, had little confidence the so-called school and its instructors knew what they were doing, and had no money for skydiving anyway. I never went back. Gaining some reward from a risky activity was a requisite for me to continue doing it.

I suffered a couple of serious medical errors while at State. The first was a dental surgical error. My wisdom teeth needed extraction. Having no cash, I went to the UNC School of Dentistry. The surgery was performed under anesthesia, but I woke up when the dental student busted up an impacted tooth with a hammer and chisel. The violent extraction left a large and inflamed wound requiring stitches. These were removed later, or so I thought. The wound failed to heal, my breath stunk like death, and after a week I became suspicious. A flashlight and some prodding revealed an overlooked stitch. This could have resulted in a severe infection. I didn't want to return to the dental hacks, so I cleaned and sterilized my roach-clip hemostat and some sharp scissors. While my roommate held the flashlight, I removed the stitch. The wound healed.

The second error was worse. I ached for female companionship. State's large male population competed for a limited number of women. My roommate Randy seemed to have no trouble, but he was highly charismatic and played the disco scene well. I wasn't, and couldn't stand discos. I went on a few dates, but I didn't know how to behave, so they were terrible, embarrassing, and didn't result in sex. My risky lifestyle was apparently insufficient to attract females. A physical problem, to my mind at least, was my scrotum held some distended veins I thought girls would find gross, and they became painful. So, I had them clipped.

The minor surgery wouldn't have been a problem, other than the area became infected. I suffered a great deal of emotional and psychological trauma regarding the potential loss of my virility. These days, I would've sued.

I returned to the urological hack who'd cut me and received large doses of antibiotics, which addressed the infection. The area was so painful, though, I couldn't stand up straight. Smoking weed made the situation worse, as I couldn't help but think about my damaged and aching scrotum. Walter hooked me up with speedball, a combination of cocaine and heroin historically used for the palliative care of terminal cancer patients. The cocktail has killed some famous people who injected it recreationally. I snorted this potent analgesic, and all pain left my body. I cared about nothing, and just lay on my bed buzzing away.

After this episode, I resolved to stay away from opiates and synthetic opioids to the degree possible and simply suck up the pain. The opiate high felt *too* good, and I knew these drugs were physically addictive. Fortunately, I didn't have any functional impairment after this infection, but it presaged later issues.

For many students, an undergraduate university education opens doors to a successful career and life. Not for me, at least not immediately. Graduate school would one day fulfill this goal. However, one undergraduate course did stick to my ribs. It was called Social Ecology.

The instructor was an animated and knowledgeable fellow who was far ahead of his time. It was the only course I enjoyed stoned, and I did well in it.

One of the required readings was *The Limits to Growth* by Donella H. Meadows and others, a highly prescient book. It describes one of the first examples of large-scale system computer simulation modeling, applied to humans' interactions with the Earth. Many years later, I met one of the authors at a system dynamics conference, and I told him the work changed the way I viewed the world and macro-scale risk. The concepts that humanity was on a suicidal course unless it constrained itself, and that risk could be simulated on a computer (at the time, employing vacuum tubes and punch cards) resonated with me.

I've read less-than-thoughtful critiques claiming the book's conclusions were incorrect, as economic and societal collapse has yet to happen. Who cares if they were off a few years? "All models are wrong but some models are useful," is a wise quote attributed to the statistician George Box. Collapse will happen, given a lack of substantive action to prevent it.

Reading *The Limits to Growth* cracked open an important intellectual door.

As my tenure at State and the seventies came to a close, I had no particular plan for the next stage of my life. I graduated with a decent grade-point average, but I didn't have a practical degree. Some friends had jobs lined up and some applied to graduate school. All I wanted was to be in the wilderness and out of the South.

My friends Dick and Dave had somehow found logging jobs in southeast Alaska the previous summer, and came back telling tales of wild country, wild animals, and wild men. The lifestyle sounded appealing, so I called their employer, and he said, "Come on up." I sold my stereo for a one-way ticket to Juneau.

This was a risky move, but the Alaskan door was a wild one.

The Grunt Work Door

I'M A TIRED, COLD, WET SPONGE. MY CO-WORKERS ARE LOSERS, ADDICTS, and criminals who work hard, nonetheless. Most are always stoned on something. I'm encased in rubber from head to toe, with wool underneath. The smell of wet vegetation permeates everything. It's always raining, and never warm. I'm in virgin wilderness, moss-covered primordial forest never seen by humans. The streams are choked with salmon during spawning. Some days, I see a dozen or so nine-foot-plus Alaskan brown bears, thousand-pound monsters who have never seen humans and who're afraid of absolutely nothing. They can kill with one swipe of their eight-inch wide paws, armed with claws like curved daggers. I carry a bolt-action rifle chambered for .375 H&H Magnum 300 grain bullets for bear defense. I'm reluctant, but I slosh through the door to woods work.

Upon arrival in Ketchikan, I was told no logging jobs were available. Many people who work for or with the US Forest Service refer to the agency as the *Forest Circus*. The logger I spoke to explained he hadn't won an expected Circus contract, and he'd had to lay off workers. This put me in a bit of a sticky wicket, as I had no return ticket and little money. If this had happened later in life when I was more confident, I would've wrested a return ticket out of the man. My life, however, would've proceeded in a completely different direction, so I'm glad I didn't wrest anything.

The lack of logging jobs was actually a fortunate turn, as logging is particularly dangerous. I flew back to Juneau, where there were other jobs. I worked for a few months for minimum wage in a Forest Circus visitor's center at Mendenhall Glacier, a stop for busloads of well-heeled cruise ship tourists. I couldn't afford rent. I'd expected to live in a logging camp, but I was able to use temporary government housing in Juneau.

The only people who lived in Juneau seemed to be those who didn't fit in anywhere else. Fishermen and loggers came into town and blew their entire paychecks drinking and whoring. The town smelled like fishy moss, or mossy fish. Bald eagles dumpster-dove, competing with the ravens. It felt like time travel back to a wilder era.

Tiring of cleaning up tourist trash and actual crap, I capitalized on a forestry course I took at State, and switched to a surveying job. Surveying in those conditions wasn't any more pleasant than logging, but at least the work itself was easier and a bit safer. Survey crews laid out the boundaries of future logging areas in virgin wilderness with compasses and *chains* (long tape measures). This was way before Global Positioning Systems (GPS). Once logged, the areas are called *clear-cuts*. All marketable trees are felled, then skidded down to the ocean and floated to mills. Surveying was my introduction to woods work.

The crew flew from town to the field camps in small float planes, flown by crazy-ass bush pilots whose idea of fun was diving toward and buzzing whales, mere feet above the waves. The camps looked like sets from the Robert Altman movie *M.A.S.H.* Miserable workers living in miserable canvas tents in miserable, sopping wet forest. We suffered from gastrointestinal illness much of the time, due to fecal contamination or *camp crud.* It was difficult to obtain fresh food except for fish.

We flew to the survey line most days in Vietnam-era Bell *Huey* helicopters, piloted by freaky Vietnam vets who were usually drunk or stoned. Decapitation during loading was a concern for tall people like me. Crosswinds off the glaciers above the forest zone pummeled the aircraft. The helicopters pitched and yawed wildly once they took off and rose above the treetops. None of us ate breakfast before going to work. The pilots yelled at us in our headsets to shut up so they could concentrate in such conditions.

The pilots often landed in muskeg, as these were the only open areas. Few things were more unpleasant than stepping out into a bog and sinking down, *OTT* or over-the-top of our knee-high rubber boots, into the cold peaty water. Then we'd have to take off our helmets and reeking, fireproof onesies with the rotor screaming in our ears.

I was concerned about some of the workers carrying rifles. Many had never hunted or even fired a weapon, yet the government handed them powerful firearms used to hunt the largest game on Earth. Training for shooting a charging bear, dodging-and-weaving through thick forest, consisted of the crew chief setting up a stationary cardboard box fifty feet away and instructing the shooter to fire away. Fortunately, nobody on my crew ever shot a bear or human. Capsaicin bear spray, a much more effective defensive weapon, had yet to be invented.

Much of the work involved just making it through the day without getting killed by ursine monsters or other means, or going rain insane. Everybody had different coping mechanisms. Being in a stoned state made the work less pleasant for me, as the days seemed much too long, and I tended to focus on my physical misery. I'd wait until I was in the tent at night to light up. I felt overwhelming relief lying stoned next to a glowing wood stove in a dry tent.

Working in such unpleasant surroundings, with many unpleasant people, required a simultaneous mix of inward retreat and congeniality. I'd done plenty of hard work before this, but not at such a high level of wretchedness.

There were, however, occasional moments of transcendence. As long as I accepted the suffering, there were fine rewards: Spawning female salmon leaping over dams of their dead and rotting sisters who didn't make it. A gigantic brownie, sitting on his haunches eating caviar from the gravid belly of a salmon he'd just snagged and ripped open with a single claw. Impromptu sight-seeing tours over pristine fjords, provided by the heli pilots when they had extra fuel. Keeping my shit together while hiking, camping, and tripping on psychedelics on my days off; lever-action Guide Gun on my pack or next to my sleeping bag, loaded for big bear. Hikes along wild beaches choked with giant driftwood, making way for the occasional lumbering bear. Glorious views of the Juneau Icefield and the coastline, achieved by *bushwhacking* (trail-less hiking through bush, which whacks the bushwhacker) and *scrambling* (easy, un-roped rock climbing) up unclimbed and unnamed peaks on rare, precipitation-free off days. My first aurora borealis, witnessed on a rare clear night from the deck of a ferry plying between islands, miles from any shore lights. It was astounding. A yellow-green corona originating from overhead like divine rays of love, an LSD trip without drugs.

None of us thought the surveyed areas would ever be logged, given the remoteness of the work sites, but we were wrong. Complete islands were logged, for example, with a thin screen of trees left standing at the water's edge so the aftermath of forest rape wouldn't upset the cruise ship and ferry passengers. From the air, they looked like the pates of bald men with a fringe of hair. Logging in Southeast Alaska was, historically, a sad tale of ecologically devastating and economically ignorant forest resource management. It's fortunate some of the forest was preserved before it was all destroyed. Some still want to destroy it.

I saved enough money to travel to Denali National Park (Mt. McKinley at the time), with an ecologist from Oregon whom I'd met in Juneau. We had good weather, and the tundra's fall colors were psychedelic, set off by recent snows on the panorama of the Alaska Range. We didn't climb, but sought out bears and other wildlife, sneaking unarmed into wildlife-rich areas so he could get good photos.

It was an amazing introduction to the Alaska Range. However, as winter approached, I decided I'd had my fill of Alaska. It's bad enough in the summer; the winter is, well . . . tough. My friend extended an invitation to visit in Corvallis, Oregon. If nothing else, I could get a job tree-planting in the Oregon Coast Range and Cascades. I could indeed find nothing else.

Some areas I planted in Oregon and Washington were almost entirely logged as far as I could see. It appeared as if the forests had been carpet-bombed into oblivion. The *slash* (vegetative debris) and understory vegetation in clear-cuts were typically burned to make way for the next crop of trees. As opposed to diverse old-growth forests, this was a form of monoculture, usually with fast-growing Douglas Fir. In some cases, clear-cuts were still steaming in the rain when the planters arrived to establish the next crop, enhancing the battle-zone appearance. Many of the areas I planted had been old-growth forest, soil hidden from the light of day for thousands of years.

Tree-planters had to be strong, fit, and motivated. They were some tough dudes, such as out-of-work or out-of-season loggers and wildland firefighters. Everybody carried knives, so you needed to be careful about pissing others off. It was a brutal job, involving rapid mucking about on steep muddy hillsides over slimy logs and through bush, carrying twenty or more pounds of wet baby trees in a bag on your hips and a Neolithic-type digging tool called a *hoedad* in your hand. Hoedads were another reason I didn't want to piss off other planters.

The task involved cleaving a small slot in the ground with the hoedad, flicking the baby tree roots into the hole, stomping on it, and hoping it grew. Baboons could do it. Any human with a lick of sense either never does it, or only does it for a short time. It's a job of last resort, although a life of petty or violent crime might be lower on the scale of desirable work. Imagine hiking as fast as you can through heavy bush, up steep hills in the cold rain, covering thousands of feet of elevation per day, day after long, working day. Tree-planting was worse.

In order to make good money in this piecework job, a planter had to plant a thousand or more trees per day. The crews worked from dawn to dusk, however long that might be. Most of the work in the Oregon Coast Range was in the winter, but I could plant most of the year by moving around. Some days I planted over two thousand trees. Over a period of three years, working, on average, eight-month seasons, I planted hundreds of thousands of trees. If even a fraction of these grew, I did my good citizen's part in offsetting carbon emissions, if nothing else. Forestry surveying was difficult, but tree-planting was a different beast altogether.

My first planting job was on a largely gay crew out of Corvallis. It took me a while to realize their orientation, as these guys were tough and I was naïve, despite the fact I'd known some macho gay and bi athletes at State. They never approached or threatened me in a sexual sense, but were physically friendly with each other. I don't know whether they self-identified as gay or not. The orientation of the planters didn't bother me, but I just didn't fit in.

Although I was fit in a cardio sense when I started, I was also weak, slow and inexperienced. The torture imposed upon the newbie by the crew chief involved ordering me to carry bags of trees from a *landing* (parking area) out to the planters. This was torturous in several respects: The tree-packer was the bottom rung in the male hierarchical ladder. Wet bags of trees weighed twenty or more pounds each, and I had to carry one on each shoulder; my body only weighed one-seventy. I didn't have a hoedad to help stabilize myself on the steep hills. My floppy Juneau rubber boots were useless, and I couldn't afford good work boots until I'd saved enough money.

I spent much of my time falling in the mud, scraping and bruising my body on the slash, and being laughed at. It's a wonder I didn't break any bones. I don't know why I didn't quit. I was bullheaded, I suppose, but I also didn't have many employment alternatives at the time.

My solution to this unpleasant situation? I learned to move faster and convinced the crew chief to let me start planting. I also gained weight and strength, bought good boots, and learned to move more efficiently over rough terrain. I had three advantages: good cardio, long legs, and ambidexterity. Recall, I was a forced right-hander. For tree-planting, being able to use both arms meant more endurance as a switch-planter, shifting the heavy hoedad from hand to hand to avoid fatigue. Switching also avoided *logger's claw*, hand cramping resulting from gripping a cold tool handle for long periods in cold rain.

I switched crews once I became competent, and escaped a male tribe to which I didn't belong. I quickly reckoned that not only could I make more money, I could avoid getting caught in the horrific bush and slash by rapidly planting the *cat* (bulldozer) roads at the edges of clear-cuts. I'd jump out of the *crummy* (a 1970s or '80s four-wheel-drive or 4WD vehicle) running and switch-backing up the cat roads. Jumping-the-gun pissed off the other planters who got stuck with the slash, but tree-planting was a pure performance-driven activity. The fastest were paid and respected the most.

This period was the first time since childhood I'd eaten a decent diet, as I was making enough money to pay for it. I knew I needed to eat well to work like a mule on meth. I gained weight and attained a lean two hundred pounds.

Being subjected to masculine pack and tribal behavior at a primal level was challenging. The closest analogue to what I experienced planting might have been that of a convict labor culture. I've never been imprisoned, but some of my co-workers were ex-cons and confirmed my observation.

It was necessary for the crew chief to be a large, strong, confident man who could kick ass. Otherwise, the hierarchy wouldn't work. Below him, the hierarchy was established by size, strength, speed, and intimidation.

Having a sense of humor helped a lot. Planters could survive by being inconspicuous, but this wouldn't have worked in my case.

I was proud I never got into a real fight. Nobody ever touched me, except for handshakes. Most planters weren't so fortunate; there were many beatings. Knives were sometimes pulled. Nobody was hoedad-ed, though. On the lower rungs of the ladder, planters simply tried to maintain and survive. I occasionally stepped in and protected the omegas. I couldn't abide bullying. There were occasional female planters, but most didn't last long. I wouldn't have wanted to have been in their situation.

The crew chief was the alpha. I never wanted alpha-dom. I was the beta baboon. I made over twenty dollars per hour in the early 1980s, often under-the-table, which was great for such menial work. I'd also never been in a situation of competence and respect, aside from making good grades. This albeit slight reward may help explain why I planted for the next three years.

I was homeless part of the time. We stayed in cheap hotels and camps during most contracts. I learned to maintain and indeed have fun while working in awful conditions, and I saw a lot of the Pacific and Mountain West.

I planted my way through the door of keeping a good attitude and my shit together in tough conditions.

I also made some good friends. Doug, the alpha crew chief, a Montanan my height, but thirty pounds heavier. He was a gentle bear of a man who worked as a wildland firefighting crew chief in the summers. He could've picked me up and body-slammed me without breaking a sweat. Bob, taller than me, lean as a whippet, and a sex addict. If it moved and he could catch it, he'd bonk it. Grant, a well-read and funny fellow who married Doug's sister and became a grade school-teacher. Barry, the crew drug dealer, who once cooked up some potent hashish brownies for the last day of a contract, resulting in a sort of search-and-rescue operation for some severely stoned planters at the end of the day. Working with interesting and entertaining people who didn't whine made a big difference in such work.

Then there were those who were less-than-friends. Wolfman, a diminutive drunk and opiate addict. He had an unfortunate tendency to challenge dudes much larger than himself in bars and get his ass kicked, thus explaining his scarred and broken visage. I once walked in on him and two other dudes getting all jiggy in bed with a whore. Perhaps they got a volume discount.

Joe, an ex-Marine dishonorably discharged for almost killing another Marine with his fists. He seemed proud of this. I had to shut him down once in a crowded bar. He was goading me for reasons unclear. I threatened, in a loud voice, "If you don't shut the fuck up, I'm going to pin you and shove that Bud bottle up your ass." He shut the fuck up.

There were a few Vietnam vets who, in general, were a severely screwed-up lot. This was the first time I witnessed intravenous drug use, which repelled me. It crossed a pharmaceutical red line. In retrospect, I should've had more sympathy for them, but I only had so much good will to spread around.

As long as the hierarchy was maintained, a forced but mutually support- ive society existed. If somebody quit or wasn't able to work, the rest of us were required to work harder, but sometimes planters just couldn't take it anymore. For example, a couple of Oregon guys who were pioneering tech- nical rock climbers threw down their tools on a few foul weather days, ran down the hill, and hitchhiked into town. They reappeared a few days later begging for work. This bailing-and-returning behavior amused Doug and I, and we'd make fun of the tough-guy climbers who couldn't take a little tree-planting. Little did I know I'd become one of those technical climbers later in life. Planting was excellent training for mountaineering.

While planting with Doug's crew in western Montana for three sea- sons, a vermiculite plant near Libby was spitting asbestos into the air. They manufactured material used for potting soil, packing material, and the like. We were unaware of our potential asbestos exposure. If I ever get mesotheli- oma, asbestos exposure is the probable cause, although the cancer would've shown up by now.

In 1980, Mt. St. Helens blew up, dusting western Montana and turn- ing everything ghostly gray. Nobody seemed to know whether the ash was toxic, although it seemed to me that inhaling lungfuls of silicaceous volca- nic ash wasn't healthy. An official state of emergency was declared, and the state closed all the bars. Horrors! We had nothing better to do than to drive back to Oregon—challenging, given the closure of many highways. Since dust masks immediately sold out, we wore bandanas over our faces. This did little to reduce ash inhalation, but it gave us the raffish appearance of an ashy gang of desperadoes.

Getting to and from the work sites was often risky. Maneuvering a large 4WD vehicle with up to eight people in it, up and down logging roads in various states of disrepair, was dangerous in itself. Even turning around could be problematic. Overloaded logging trucks with sketchy brakes barreling down twisty muddy roads around blind corners added to the excitement. Large wildlife jumping in front of the vehicle added even more. Flat tires weren't uncommon, but thankfully we never had a blowout while moving. Trees and rocks could block the roads, although eight strong guys could deal with these pretty quickly.

These vehicular concerns applied not only to woods work, but also to approaching wilderness areas in ranges such as the Oregon and Washington Cascades. Ever since then, I always carry a shovel, machete, ax, saw, large jack, and lots of other tools and repair materials in whatever wilderness-access vehicle I own.

The tree-planters themselves had a prudent rule that the crummy driver could be stoned but not drunk. Stoners tend to be careful drivers. After one long day, Grant was the designated stoned driver. He was driving back from the work site on a highway after dark at what he considered to be a safe speed. We saw the lights of a Montana state trooper behind us and jettisoned several joints out the windows. The cab of the crummy could've been featured in a Cheech and Chong movie, it was so up in smoke. We also had a couple of twelve-packs going.

Grant rolled down his window a few inches, and asked in a shaky vibrato, "What appears to be the problem, officer?"

The trooper replied, "Son, can you explain to me why you are driving ten miles below the legal speed limit of fifty-five miles an hour?"

Fortunately, Doug knew the cop, and leaned over from the passenger seat to explain we were all tired, and we'd drive closer to the speed limit.

The trooper seemed satisfied, and advised, "Well, you boys be careful now." As soon as he left, the crummy echoed with gales of laughter. Grant sped it up.

A systemic change occurred in my final planting season. Tree-planting contractors discovered they could hire illegal Mexican immigrants at a fraction of the wages of non-immigrants. I found these guys a joy to work with.

They'd sing in Spanish while working in thirty-five degrees and pouring rain. It was time to move on, regardless.

What's worse than tree-planting? Hauling a thick, heavy, thousand-foot hose through clear-cuts spraying hundreds of gallons of glyphosate, or Roundup. A forest products company reckoned it was more cost-effective to apply massive amounts of the herbicide to freshly logged clear-cuts to kill the undergrowth, as opposed to burning and clearing the slash. Thus, Doug and a business partner hit upon a unique market.

It wasn't possible to perform aerial spraying. The chemical might have drifted and killed nearby forests and polluted streams. It took too much time to use backpack sprayers. We even thought about using large helium balloons to lift the hose, but this would've been a disaster in a high wind. So, Doug and I would park a large tank truck at the bottom or top of a clear-cut and drag the giant hose, dousing the vegetation. We didn't have the advantage of a hoedad to help us up the hills, and we were often forced to crawl through tall piles of slash. Both hands were needed to handle the heavy hose and nozzle. This made acrobatics necessary. Clouds of mosquitos and flies tormented us, this being during the summer growing season.

We were exposed to large amounts of industrial strength glyphosate, which sounds awful, but this was probably not problematic as Roundup is designed to kill plants, not mammals. Any adverse effects would've shown up by now. We wore no respiratory protection; it would've been impossible to work fast in such gear. We'd soak ourselves and our clothing with liberal amounts of Vietnam-surplus, almost hundred percent N,N-diethyl-meta-toluamide (DEET), or *jungle juice*. It also wasn't very toxic, although it melted some forms of plastic.

Spraying the clear-cuts didn't last long, which was fortunate. I have extensive scarring on my shins from the slash, to remind me. At least Doug and I didn't have to deal with the baboonish interpersonal dynamics associated with tree-planting.

Doug and others tried to get me into wildland or forest firefighting, but this dangerous job crossed a red line for me. My aversion was well warranted based on subsequent reports from former firefighters. The obvious risks included flying, jumping out of planes, and working around and in massive out-of-control fires. Wildland firefighters also inhale smoke on a continuous basis, with little or no respiratory protection; as in spraying, such protection makes it almost impossible to work. Smoke from burning wood is not only unpleasant, it causes a variety of serious chronic ailments. Glad I didn't go there. Most of the firefighters I knew smoked cigarettes, as if they didn't inhale enough smoke already.

I had little enthusiasm for exploring the forests and mountains during my woods work period, since I already spent so much time working outdoors. Time off in the company of female companions inside warm dry houses was more appealing.

Regardless, I went on some memorable trips. I was completely alone for more than a week on an early spring, solo trek across Oregon's Three Sisters Wilderness. I hiked on reflective snowpack, the sun blazing the entire time. By the end of the week, my exposed skin was fried. After this, I was much more careful with sunblock, although it didn't help my already red neck. Sunglasses at the time weren't effective in blocking ultraviolet radiation, so I hope my eyes haven't suffered from such exposure.

My only whitewater paddling experience occurred around this time. A friend convinced me to join him on a canoe trip on the frigid McKenzie River in Oregon. I don't know the degree of technical difficulty of the rapids we shot, but the water seemed pretty turbulent to me. He was experienced, or so he said. He barked orders at me from the stern while we furiously paddled.

We were fine for a while, but we then hit a large rock and overturned. My first concern was losing my glasses, as I wore no retainer. I should've been more concerned about our lack of floatation vests and helmets, but this wasn't common practice at the time. Perhaps paddlers were more buoyant and had thicker skulls back then. We managed to avoid drowning and hauled the canoe to shore. We were both hypothermic and shivered uncontrollably, but the day was warm and sunny. We needed to paddle out to reach a vehicle we'd parked down-stream, but had no more mishaps. That was it for me. Like skydiving, it was unpleasant and unrewarding.

I was spit out on the beach by the whitewater river adventure door. I'm sure rafting, kayaking, and other water sports have their rewards for some, but also I chose to limit my cumulative risk, particularly given my poor swimming skills and tendency to sink in fresh water.

While tree-planting, I rented cheap houses in Corvallis with housemates or girlfriends. I didn't own a car, so I either borrowed their cars or rode my bike. The terrain of the Willamette Valley is mostly flat, so cycling was an easy way to get around. Like any cyclist, I'd experienced my share of close calls with vehicles, but one incident in particular pedaled me out of the cycling door.

I was cruising along on a nice wide country road, heading home from a visit to town, when a pickup truck almost hit me at high speed. The passenger tossed a beer bottle out of the window as the truck passed me. I wasn't wearing head protection, as good helmets hadn't yet been invented. The bottle missed my head by inches. I offered the truck the universal symbol of displeasure, an emphatic middle finger. The truck's brake lights fired up, it squealed to a stop, and two big bubbas jumped out.

One growled, "We're gonna kick your faggot ass."

I replied, picking up my bike, "Bring it on. I'll wrap this fucking bike around both your fucking red necks."

Somewhat surprisingly, the threat worked, and they retreated, mumbling something about me being a "freak."

Fortunately, I had no other such episodes, at least while cycling. I later stopped cycling altogether when I began to develop chronic numbness in my crotch, a highly disturbing outcome. Cycling is a high-risk activity anywhere other than designated bike paths, due to potential automotive interactions. Off-road cycling is just as risky. I've known more people injured from falls and crashes while mountain biking than any other outdoor sport, but it attracts many people.

Of course, cycling risk doesn't compare to motorcycles. From a risk perspective, motorcycles are essentially bicycles ridden at highway speed in vehicular traffic. Motorcycle crashes are much more likely to result in death compared to car crashes, as the vehicles offer minimal protection from injury. They probably wouldn't be legal if they were invented in recent times.

I traveled to tree-planting jobs in crummies, but I'd hitchhike between jobs to go hiking or climbing, or just to visit friends. I'd been hitching since I was a teen. Hitching was risky back then, but I can't imagine what it's like now. It involved an unlikely bond of trust between the hitchee and the hitcher, both subject to robbery or worse.

I was picked up once in Montana, and the driver revealed as I got in, "I've got a forty-five here, so don't try anything."

"Well, I've got a six-inch hunting knife here, so we're even," I replied.

He busted out laughing and invited me to roll a joint from a large stash of weed in his glove compartment. Weed was usually a good icebreaker or ride payment, except for the times when a driver was drunk or falling asleep and wanted me to drive. That was an interesting risk-risk tradeoff on the part of the driver.

I indeed carried a hunting knife and would've willingly planted it in an attacker's crotch, but never had to pull it. Everyone who ever picked me up, over dozens of trips, was cool. There were a couple of rides with holy rollers who preached to me, but I ignored them and just nodded my head now and then.

While in Corvallis, I escaped woods work for a time by earning an undergraduate teaching degree from Oregon State University. I was a student teacher in a remote Yupik village in western Alaska, through an exchange program. The main risks in the village were extreme cold, boredom, the potential for killing yourself driving a snowmobile at high speed, and the copious amounts of drugs and alcohol consumed by the largely White teachers. The White teachers appeared to fall into two camps divided among schools: either devoutly religious or hearty partiers. I could hang with the latter group, but it drained me. I was offered a teaching job in the village at a high salary, and I liked the Yupik people, but the overall setting was just too alien for me.

Corvallis was a center for growing grass seed, so I felt horrible due to allergies when the grass flowered. Plus I wanted to be near bigger mountains. I moved to Bellingham, Washington in 1983. The main risk in Bellingham at the time was being overwhelmed by the foul stench of a pulp mill. Bellingham's cleaned up since then.

I substitute taught for a short time in the public schools. I thought being a teacher in Washington and having summers off in the North Cascades would be a great gig, but I didn't have the patience or temperament for such a stressful job. Being back in high school in a position of authority was uncomfortable. My previous jobs involved just showing up and doing the job well, and teaching involves great responsibility, although teachers aren't paid accordingly. As most people can attest, there's a great deal of assholery on the part of high school students, and I just can't abide assholes.

My escape from the woods was therefore short-lived. I returned to forestry and other types of surveying. As opposed to the crude surveying in Alaska, this work was just as difficult, but required a greater degree of technical knowledge and experience. There was also a great deal of rain and misery.

I worked for a company that accepted contracts nobody else wanted. Easier work was rare during the early 1980s era of economic recession in the Pacific Northwest. This was before Microsoft and other tech companies took off. Old-growth forest logging sighed its last gasps in a sad final act of ecological devastation.

We surveyed a remote wild area of the North Cascades targeted for logging. This area was later designated as a US Forest Service Wilderness Area, so all our work was for naught, but that was fine with me. Three of us packed in our surveying and camping gear, and hundreds of wooden stakes to delineate a potential old-growth forest area slated to be clear-cut. The contract was the only time I ever carried a backpack weighing over a hundred pounds.

It was a stunning area to work in, until it snowed a couple of feet one night. It was one of my first experiences dealing with somebody who was freaking out and letting fear take hold. This surprised me because he was ex-Army and had Black Belts in three different martial arts disciplines. The snow threatened to collapse his cheap tent and he was cold. My solution? Tell him to beat the snow off his tent walls, heat up some soup, smoke a joint, and shut up so I could sleep, which surprisingly worked. The next day, we plodded out with heavy loads in heavy wet snow. We all agreed we could leave the hundreds of wooden stakes without guilt.

Surveying in that area paled in comparison to resurveying about ten miles of a remote area bordering Mt. Rainier National Park. The Forest Service had allowed a contractor to log bordering forest up to the National

Park boundary, and the contractor cut some large old-growth trees within the Park. Whoops. Large trees such as these were quite valuable, but this was theft and resulted in large fines.

Jerry and I followed the original survey notes and markers from the early 1900s. It was interesting detective work, but the terrain was bushy, trail-less, and brutally steep. I wore out two pairs of expensive work boots in a summer. We had to cross the Carbon River to access much of the area, which meant crossing a raging, braided, glacial river twice a day. We'd try to cross on downed logs, or we'd move logs, but sometimes we had to suffer through icy, thigh-deep water crossings after taking off our pants and boots.

Once we had surveyed the area, we returned with four-foot aluminum posts to hammer in every hundred feet along the boundary. We had to cross the river repeatedly, but this time with fifty-pound shoulder-loads of posts. Amazingly, Jerry and I never lost our footing in the river.

Jerry was an alcoholic and cigarette smoker who prowled the bars most every night. He began his days puking and then lighting up. We worked an average of twelve-hour days, six days per week, for months. I told Jerry, "Man, if you cleaned up, you could be an Olympic athlete."

Surveying in the snow was less-than inspiring. For example, we snowmobiled into a National Forest area, due to the Circus's desire to survey clear-cut boundaries so spring logging could begin as soon as the snow melted. The boss's strapping redneck brother was the crew-chief-for-the-day. We arrived at the site, and he trudged off randomly through thigh-deep snow, tripping every few feet on buried stumps and logs and face-planting. I told him he didn't know where the hell he was going, and somebody was going to get hurt. Things got testy. I took off along the correct line, post-holing as fast as I could in the deep snow. He and the others caught up half an hour later, and he apologized.

Surveying in the ocean was also less-than inspiring. I had to hold a mirror steady while bobbing about in an inflatable Zodiac in three-foot chop, reflecting a laser from the theodolite on the shore. This established a plot for crab harvesting. Whenever Jerry on the theodolite yelled in my earpiece, I dropped a cinderblock tied to a buoy. Yet another job that didn't allow me to eat breakfast beforehand. At least I wore a floatation vest.

Subsequent jobs were physically easier, but sometimes riskier. Some people get red-faced irate about their property rights, which is fine as long as they know where their property ends. A rural landowner constructed a half-mile fence in the wrong location, about ten feet into his neighbor's land. The neighbor called us to establish the correct location of the fence.

While setting stakes along the correct property line, I looked up and saw six Dobermans charging toward me. I carried a hatchet I used for hammering the stakes and a machete for clearing brush. In my experience dogs won't attack somebody who isn't displaying fear and who has weapons. They aren't stupid.

I stood my ground, and the dogs did the same, barking and snarling several yards from me. As I considered my next move, the corpulent landowner sauntered out with a semi-auto twelve-gauge.

He aimed the gun at me and demanded, "What the hell you doing on my property?"

I yelled back, "Sir, I'm not on your property. You built your fence in the wrong location. I have a legal right to be here. If you don't call off your dogs, I'm going to turn them into hamburger, and if you don't stop pointing your fucking gun at me, I'm coming after you next."

He called me crazy, retreated, and yelled that he'd call the county sheriff, who appeared later. We completed the work without the presence of the Cujos and Shotgun Neighbor, the sheriff keeping a watchful eye. I declined to press assault charges. I don't know why I felt magnanimous. I hope I never have such a neighbor. I also hope nobody ever points a bloody gun at me again. It pisses me off to no small degree.

I had some other close encounters of the violent kind during my surveying years, including with co-workers. For example, Cletus, a big powerlifter, threatened my friend Buddy over some perceived disrespect. Buddy suffered from severe scoliosis and had a Harrington metal rod clamped to his spine.

Cletus spat, "I'm going to break that fucking rod in your back."

I stood in front of Buddy and loudly spat back, "If you fucking touch him, I'll pin you in front of everybody here and shove your fucking plumb bob up your ass."

This means of intimidation, as in the ex-Marine case earlier, was effective. Cletus shut up and never threatened Buddy again. I'm glad such threats worked, but I wouldn't have made them had I not been ready to carry them out.

The riskiest aspect of urban surveying involved working in the middle of roads and highways with only a magic, orange plastic cone force-field to protect me from the multi-ton vehicles whizzing by. Brightly colored safety clothing was not standard issue at the time. There were some close calls.

Standing in the middle or on the shoulder of roads required a sort of inner retreat and focus. I couldn't use the instruments and concentrate on getting the work over with as soon as possible if I was distracted by the possibility of certain death zooming by only a few feet away. Even as a kid, I thought the conventional wisdom regarding "walk, don't run" across a street to be unwise. The less time spent in a perilous situation, the better. Driving a car is highly risky, but standing in traffic without a substantial metal enclosure is a little more disconcerting. Getting a risky job over with as soon as possible and back to relative safety was good training for harder climbing.

Working around heavy equipment was also risky, especially if, say, the shovel operator had hit the sauce at lunchtime. An amusing accusatory comment I often heard on construction sites was, "Sumpin' don't look right," as if the surveyors' measurements were somehow less accurate than the judgement of a drunk driver at the controls of a giant earthmoving machine.

Surveying was mildly interesting work, and the pay was decent, but we attempted to make it more entertaining. Good people made all the difference.

Jerry could've been a stand-up comic. He developed his sense of humor to avoid going bonkers from being deployed for long periods on the *USS Enterprise* during the Vietnam War.

Hank, an ex-Marine Native American, was equally funny. He may have been unique among surveyors because he was red-green colorblind, which made things difficult for him. Surveyors depend on being able to distinguish red and orange flagging, for example. I think he just considered it a challenge.

Hank and I would have contests to see who could push over the biggest dead trees in the woods, and how fast we could cut down trees with machetes. He claimed chainsaws were for wimps, but in reality, we just didn't want to pack them in. We engaged in other admittedly silly male contests to entertain ourselves, such as who could remove asphalt-sealed manhole covers the fastest by wailing on them with a sledgehammer. Hank was, however, an astute fellow, and the source of wise advice that has guided my life in many respects ever since.

Once, when I was cussin' at a misbehaving theodolite, he observed, "Robert, you just have to be smarter than the equipment."

Both Jerry and Hank were expert surveyors who were smarter than the equipment, and they took pride in their work. GPS was just starting to be used when I retired from surveying. We didn't need no stinkin' GPS, and I've never used it in the wilderness. I learned much from those men; practical wilderness navigation and keeping a good attitude in difficult conditions.

Such work was seasonal. In the off-season, I'd take whatever back-breaking work I could find. The worst job was one in which I did nothing but shovel pea gravel for drainage at a new condo development. I used a shovel with a steel pipe for a handle; wooden handles broke with the strain.

I helped demolish buildings, remodel houses, and move houses by hauling them on a large flatbed; nasty, dangerous work. I wore no personal protective equipment aside from gloves. Nobody did. I didn't think about it much, and regulations were lax in those days. So, I wasn't always consistent with regard to rational risk management, but this situation demonstrates tribal influence on risk management practices. Grunt labor is a tribe in which members influence each other with regard to managing risk.

As an alternative career, I heard about a job with a nonprofit, outdoor learning program based in Seattle, similar to Outward Bound. It sounded intriguing. The clients were juvenile offenders, so the leaders referred to the program, inappropriately I thought, as "Hoods in the Woods." The intent, as far as I could determine, was to take the kids into the Cascades backcountry in the winter and make them cold, wet, and unhappy. Somehow, this was supposed to improve their attitudes.

In my interview, the head instructor asked whether I'd gone through Outward Bound, the National Outdoor Leadership School, or a similar program—or better yet, if I'd been an instructor. I replied no, but told him I'd done a shitload of hard, outdoor work and some mountaineering, and had a teaching degree. This didn't seem to give me much cred, but he accepted me into the leader training program, probably because they were desperate.

The trips were in the winter. A requisite skill was knowing how to ski. I owned some cross-country skis, which were long, skinny, and flexible. I wore floppy leather boots clamped to bindings at the toe. This sort of rig resulted in the persistent term *pinhead* applied to free-heel or telemark skiers. The bindings had three little pins that fitted into holes in the toe of the boot sole. My skiing experience was limited to sliding along rolling trails, and I'd never tried to make sharp turns in steep terrain. The only kids I knew in North Carolina who went alpine or downhill skiing at resorts were the middle-class and rich kids. I never had the opportunity.

Turning on skis is necessary in order to control speed going downhill. Linking turns is great fun if the skier is proficient. Telemark skiing on steep terrain in the early 1980s was much more difficult for most people than alpine or downhill skiing, in which stiff boots are clamped at toe and the heel.

Pinheads proclaimed, "Free your heels and free your mind," as if making the sport more difficult for no reason was desirable. The area where the training took place was steep and covered in deep powder snow. I spent much of the time face-planting and wallowing in the snow. My mind wasn't freed by falling on my face.

For some reason, all the instructors skied with pinhead gear, even though ski-mountaineering rigs existed at the time, allowing skiers to lock in boot heels when the time came to negotiate steep downhills. A few of the other instructors could kind-of-sort-of ski on these pinhead rigs, which was impressive, but most of them kept me company with faces in the snow and butts in the air. Luckily, there were no injuries. I ended up head-down and skis-up in a deep tree well once, which can be fatal if nobody else is around. I suffered only humiliation.

Most of my so-called wilderness leadership training involved plodding through the snowy woods with a heavy pack, face-planting, and enduring unpleasant cold and wet conditions while camping. As an instructor, I would've spent all my time flailing about on non-turnable skis, while responsible for a bunch of unathletic teenage criminals flailing about on non-turnable skis. It seemed like a recipe for disaster with minimal pay. I quit before my first outing and went back to surveying. I would've never had the patience to become a mountain professional anyway.

A few years later, I heard one of these hoodied groups had to be rescued using helicopters because they ventured out in extreme avalanche conditions and became trapped. The organization went belly-up. I hope such programs have improved. Many years later, telemark gear improved, making the skis easy to turn.

I looked for mountain recreational opportunities with others, because I tired of always going solo. I learned about compelling outdoor trips organized through Western Washington University in Bellingham. I signed up for a winter snowshoeing trip to the Enchantment Lakes in the eastern Washington Cascades.

Tom, the organizer and leader of this trip, was a men's clothing salesman, but he seemed as if he knew what he was doing and had climbed Mt. Rainier and other peaks. He also cut a dapper figure, even in the rainy Washington wilderness. I once asked him how he stayed so neat and clean when I was often mud-covered.

He replied, "Robert, I walk around mud puddles, rather than through them."

Three other people signed up, one of whom had climber friends who lived in nearby Leavenworth. We stayed a couple of nights in their house, as they prepared to do something called *ice climbing*.

Fascinated by their gear and their rugged miens, I asked where they were going.

Their reply, "Canada."

I started to say, "Well, Canada's sort of a big place, could you be more specific?" They seemed so intense, I refrained. For all I knew, they could've been famous early ice climbers. They also annoyed me by playing and singing folk songs, badly.

Despite their earnestness, they sniggered when they saw my backpack, which I'd sewn myself. I based the design on early versions of internal frame packs, but it was elephantine (a photo of me wearing this beast in Africa appears later).

One dude snorted, "You think you're packing that up to the Enchantments in winter?"

I'd carried the pack surveying with a hundred pounds in it, and fifty to sixty pounds while hiking through winter snow. On the Enchanted trip, I broke trail much of the time, in deep powder, wearing my gi-normous pack. Our trip may have been one of the few times the Enchantments had been visited in midwinter. The area is crowded now, but our trek occurred long before the popularity of backcountry skiing in the Cascades. The trip would've been ridiculous with the skinny skis of the day and a big pack, especially given my lame skiing skills and previous leadership-in-face-planting experience. I would've wallowed like a turtle on its back if I'd fallen. On snowshoes, it was safer but still arduous. The area was wild and beautiful, and the only prints were ours. We spent a week getting there and exploring the basin.

I climbed with Tom on a few subsequent trips. He introduced me to the concept of roped climbing, and proper use of implements such as an ice ax and *crampons* (metal spikes mounted on the soles of boots) for hard snow and ice. He was an interesting fellow, but not a confident mountaineer despite his experience. Our climbing relationship didn't last long. However, one of the Enchantment trip participants introduced me to his friend Phil.

Phil was an experienced climber, but his main motivation for going into the mountains appeared to be getting high. We also shared a taste for good music. He knew the lyrics of many Frank Zappa tunes and would sing them on the trail as we hiked in a buzzed state. Phil had a great attitude, was funny, and he didn't freak out, my euphemism for feeling fear. He was the first recreational partner I knew who fulfilled these criteria. Some great climbers are so single-minded, they're as boring as plain oatmeal. Phil was by no means boring.

Phil also turned me on to mountaineering literature I could relate to, the writings of Joe Tasker and David Roberts, for example. These books weren't chest-thumping, jingoistic expeditionary tales. These guys were badasses doing real climbing and turning it into good writing.

I continued tripping out. The rural Bellingham area was fertile ground for Liberty Caps (Psilocybe semilanceata), one of the most potent psilocybin mushroom species. While surveying, I identified fields where they grew, then I'd return on a rainy day when nobody else was around and fill a grocery-size plastic bag in a couple of hours. I knew exactly what I was getting, which comforted me. I also knew folks who grew excellent weed and had access to other psychedelics.

Phil and I had a high old time exploring the Cascades while tripping and stoned. We summited a few peaks, but had fun just hanging out in cool, isolated spots. An example was Easy Ridge, which is on the long approach to Mt. Challenger in the North Cascades. It isn't easy to attain.

On the approach trail, an elderly horseman pondered the size of my home-made pack with a week's worth of food and gear and observed, "Like to pack heavy, doncha', son?"

My beast was in stark contrast to Phil's multi-day climbing pack, which was the size of a regular day pack. He claimed anything that didn't fit into this tiny pack constituted *group gear*, and he'd make other people carry it. Phil was smart.

We both suffered from foot problems. Mt. Challenger was a long way in by trail and off-trail, and neither one of us owned decent boots. So, rather than attempting the mountain, we just hung out on Easy Ridge for a couple of days. We ate wild blueberries and Liberty Caps, and marveled at the sublime beauty of the Cascades in sunny weather, a welcome respite from the typical rain.

Phil, a spiritual fellow, asked while our feet recovered, "How can you not believe in a Creator, when you witness such a scene?"

I countered, "I find it much more astounding this scene exists, when a Creator doesn't." Thus, the difference between faith and reality.

We never did any harder technical climbing, which was fine with me.

I still soloed on rock. I often visited the coast of Bellingham Bay, which has numerous overhanging sandstone formations with climbable pockets. I'd smoke weed, eat 'shrooms, and boulder alone for hours. This was before the routine use of *crash-pads* (originally, old mattresses) employed by modern boulderers, but I didn't have any serious falls.

A potentially fatal incident occurred when climbing with a co-worker during my gravel-shoveling and house-moving phase. Bruce had been a ski racer and was still an expert skier. He knew the great Billy Kidd. However, he'd never climbed a real mountain, so we decided to scramble up the North Twin Sister in the North Cascades. The peak is easy and has excellent rock. This was a good thing, since he wore his old, worn-out, smooth-soled work boots. We summited with no issues.

The North Twin has a large snowfield that can be descended by skiing or snowboarding, or by *glissading*. Glissading is a classic mountaineering technique in which climbers slide down the snow on their feet or butts in a controlled fashion. Essential skills are controlling speed using the spike end of an ice ax dragged in the snow, and braking to a stop by dropping and rolling over, planting the ax's pick in the snow. The procedure is termed self-arresting, which evokes the image of pointing a gun at yourself and cuffing your own wrists.

If the climber is good at it, glissading on the feet is akin to skiing with tiny skis, but the slope needs to be steep enough and the snow firm enough for such boot-skiing to work well. It's also slower than sliding on the butt due to friction. Butt-sliding is the most common means. It takes less skill and is less dependent on snow quality. It's faster though, which isn't always good and tends to rip up your pants. Later, I bought cheap rain pants to wear over my nice climbing pants to manage risk of ripping.

Bruce launched himself down the steep hard snow on his slick-soled boots, elegantly linking turns. His feat astonished me. Bruce had never glissaded, but it speaks to the value of being a good athlete and skier. I tried boot-skiing at first, but I wobbled and considered I might fall and tumble out of control. So, I sat on my butt. I carried my trusty three-foot long ice ax, which was good for that purpose, if little else. I picked up a lot of speed but was fine until I hit a bump, which sent me somersaulting down the slope at an uncontrollable velocity.

Disaster was averted due to several factors. The snow slope leveled out toward the bottom, and there were no rocks or trees to hit or holes to fall into. I rolled in a somewhat symmetrical fashion and didn't snap a leg, arm, or my neck. I also held on the ax tethered to my wrist. Had I let go, it would've impaled or flayed me. After several hundred yards of somersaulting, I slowed down enough to pull out of the roll and self-arrest. I couldn't stand up for several minutes due to dizziness.

Bruce found my performance hilarious and couldn't wait to get back and tell the work crew. Now days, he would've videoed it and posted it on YouTube. After this experience, I practiced glissading and self-arresting until I gained confidence to stop at high speed. Much later, after I learned to alpine ski, I learned to confidently glissade on my feet. Bruce would be proud.

Not all risks were associated with work and mountains during this period. On a dark and foggy night, I ate a large number of Liberty Caps, and walked to the campus of Western Washington University from my nearby rental house. There was a sequoia on campus. This magnificent tree wasn't nearly as tall as the Ancient Ones in California, but it was over a hundred feet, the lowest branches not far off the ground. I climbed to the top where the limbs thinned, above the top of the fog layer. The surrounding campus was a wondrous, dreamy vision. Street and pathway lights illuminated the fog from below. I found a branch big enough to sit on, fired up a doobie, and relaxed for a couple of hours. I felt the tree's life energy and serene power. Trees are among the most noble of organisms. Descending the fog-slickened branches was tricky, but I had no problems.

Despite my previous adverse encounters with water, I was keen to kayak in the ocean, and Bellingham was a portal to innumerable opportunities. I didn't have the money to buy a sea kayak, so I built one out of thin strips of cedar with a clear fiberglass coating. It was my first and only boat-building project, and it was beautiful. I didn't extend my explorations beyond Bellingham Bay due to the craft's instability. The design I employed resulted in a fast but tippy boat, and I was loath to practice Eskimo rolls in the cold water. I never put in when chop was present. Perhaps if I had built a more stable craft, I would have been more interested in sea kayaking, but I had too many competing interests on dry land.

One of these was sex, but sex can be risky. My main concern was unwanted pregnancy. I didn't want children, especially given my own childhood. I managed pregnancy risk by encouraging the small number of partners I had to use contraception, which all were willing to do.

However, serious diseases are associated with sex. I dated an intense woman for a few months in a monogamous relationship before she revealed she'd been a rock and jazz groupie. She'd been sexually active with dozens of musicians and non-musicians. Learning I had unprotected sex with a woman who had sex with some famous musicians, who in turn likely had dozens or hundreds of sex partners, was a shock. It concerned me, yet somehow thrilled me musically. It was perhaps my fault for not asking about her history before we started the relationship, but I learned my lesson.

The early 1980s was the beginning of the AIDS epidemic. I was unaware of the disease at the time, because I paid little attention to the news. Fortunately, the relationship yielded no viral consequences. Other sexually transmitted diseases concerned me, though. With subsequent partners, I became much more aware of reducing the disease risks associated with sex.

I bought a cheap drum kit while living in Washington. Most of my family is musical. I sang and played various instruments in a desultory fashion in choirs and school bands when I was young, but I'd always wanted to play drums in a rock and roll band. As a kid I played along with songs on the radio or records, pounding pencils or other improvised drumsticks on tables and other furniture, driving Frances nuts. Lack of money and parental support, moving around, and other priorities prevented me from learning to play actual drums.

Learning to play drums as an adult without lessons was painful, but I persevered. Associated risks included continuing involvement in the world of drugs, lifting heavy equipment, and repetitive motion injuries. However, rolling my way through the rock music door via drums changed my life in highly rewarding ways.

I also bought my first camera around this time, which provided another avenue for creative expression, as well as a way to document my risky activities.

I eventually escaped grunt Pacific Northwest woods work by moving back to North Carolina. The Chapel Hill and Raleigh area was prospering economically, and many of my college friends had good jobs, homes, nice clothes, and cool cars. I didn't quite understand that their success was due to the fact that they were responsible and had professional careers. I just needed work, but had no marketable skills aside from surveying and using muscle.

I owned a 1969 International Harvester pickup truck with a tall shell on the back, and I used this rig for work and camping. I sold my kayak, the only valuable possession I was willing to part with, and obtained my first credit card. After moving, this card took time to pay off, as the heavy International only went ten miles per gallon sucked down by its V-8.

In October 1985 I wandered back to North Carolina, driving down the coast to Northern California, through wine country and the Sierras, on through Arizona, Utah and New Mexico, and across the interminable flatlands until crossing over the Appalachians. I crammed all my belongings in the back of the truck, including the full drum kit. At night, I had to boondock in a narrow slot under the truck cap. I rolled joints with one hand while driving, chain-smoking weed along the way.

I'd visited the Oregon Coast many times, so that part of the route was comfortable and familiar. I climbed up many sea stacks, rock towers sculpted by wave action. Climbing took some care as the rock was often slimy and covered in bird doo, plus I needed to be mindful of being trapped by the tide.

The Sierras weren't familiar. I visited Yosemite and camped in the rain with some rock climbers. The routes they were climbing were far beyond my experience. I found the climbers interesting, but I wasn't inclined to wait for sunny weather to ask to join them. They probably would've laughed anyway. I was way out of my league. Some of these uber, strong-looking dudes and dudettes may have been famous.

Instead, I traveled to King's Canyon and spent several days tripping on LSD, smoking weed, scrambling peaks, and marveling at the beauty, completely at ease. I traveled off-trail, and saw nobody for a week.

I wanted more remote wilderness. I visited the Grand Canyon, but its physical scale overwhelmed me. I asked a Park Service employee about finding a wilderness experience, and he steered me to the Paria River Canyon in northern Arizona and southern Utah. Finding isolation and wilderness is certainly possible in the Grand Canyon, so I don't know why he directed me to the Paria, but after hiking the canyon I appreciated his advice. The Paria is crowded now, but at the time it was still largely unknown to the masses; the lack of guidebooks and no Internet being major factors.

At the beginning and end of the thirty-eight-mile hike, the canyon is wide. It narrows in the middle section to form a narrow slot canyon with walls several hundred feet high you can touch on both sides. The hike is through water for most of the route. Recent rain creates chest-deep pools. The main risk is flash flooding. Debris visible high on the canyon walls is dramatic evidence hikers don't want to be in narrow sections during a thunderstorm, or even during a thunderstorm occurring far upstream.

I left the International, my possessions locked in the back, at the trailhead and took off for eight days. The canyon has been run in a single day, but most people take three days or more. I allowed extra time for exploring side canyons such as Buckskin Gulch, supposedly the longest slot canyon in the world.

I climbed out of the main canyon at several points to higher ledges. I'm confident I left footprints where none had ever existed, as most of these side jaunts involved dicey friction climbing. I tried to stay on rock and not leave footprints. I felt I was somehow intruding on ancient terrain. I don't buy into the concept of karma, but I'm aware Mother Nature can kill me in many unpleasant ways if I don't respect her.

I tripped every day on increasingly larger doses of Bill the Cat blotter LSD (ack!) and smoked copious amounts of weed. The experience might as well have been on Mars; an exception to my previous multi-day tripping-avoidance rule. It was one of the wildest experiences in a lifetime of wild experiences. I saw nobody the entire time. As the great John Wesley Powell wrote of the Grand Canyon, "The landscape everywhere, away from the river, is of rock—cliffs of rock; plateaus of rock; terraces of rock; crags of rock—ten thousand strangely carved forms." The same applies to the Paria. Although there's plenty of life, geology overwhelms biology in such canyons.

A full moon shone that week, and the desert at night was otherworldly. The Paria is far from any artificial lights. After moonset, the Milky Way was a surreal wash of diamonds. It didn't rain, and so I didn't need to worry about flash floods. Nonetheless, I hurried through narrow sections offering no escape. I encountered some disconcerting areas of quicksand, but unlike the old Tarzan movies, I didn't disappear. I almost lost a shoe, however, which would've been disastrous.

I shot over twenty rolls of film. An early selfie shows a blazingly stoned dude, spliff in the side of his mouth, a man in a state of perfect contentment. I had an entire wilderness canyon to myself. I was in a flow state for more than a week.

I waded through the door to the Utah canyon country. There's no other place like it on Earth.

Getting back to the International from the far side of the canyon took some time, as there were no convenient shuttles back then. I tried to hitchhike, but this was and still is a remote area. Only a couple of beater cars passed the first day, the occupants throwing beer bottles at me. I don't know why I'm a magnet for such behavior. I flipped them off, but unfortunately neither of them screeched to a stop. I camped instead.

The next morning, a large recreational vehicle with a kind young Mormon family picked me up and took me all the way back to my truck. It felt bizarre riding in the back with two pretty blonde girls and a boy. I was filthy, smelly, and burned out from tripping for eight days. The whole family sang cheery religious songs. I was just damn grateful I got a ride.

I hiked a little in northern New Mexico, but I was running out of money, so I returned to my birth land, and shortly after, fell through the most influential door of my life.

An early selfie of a pariah in the Paria River canyon in Utah, midway through an eight-day trip (credit: R. C. Lee).

The early 1980s tree-planter in the Pasayten Wilderness, Washington. The flowing mullet, if not the beard, is perhaps an early harbinger of rock-band-dom (credit: unknown).

Second Movement: Duet (1987 to Present)

The Partner Door

I DATE A FEW WOMEN, BUT NO SPARK. AT MUSIC GIGS MOST WOMEN JUST want me to introduce them to the vocalists or guitarists. A door to a life partner manifests itself, however, when I meet Linda at a party to which we're both independently dragged. I see a tall, beautiful woman in an intricate African tie-dyed dress, fresh out of Kenya after three years in the Peace Corps. She's chatting with a couple of dudes about the bats fluttering around. I step up and steal her away. On our first date the next evening, at another party, somebody asks how long we've been married. We're engaged a week later. It's a black swan of relationships, and a door to having a partner in risk.

❦

Chapel Hill was a wealthy and expensive town, even in the 1980s. I lived by myself in a miserable cinder-block cottage in outlying Pittsboro. I'd arrived with no money, but found poor-paying construction jobs and joined my first real rock band.

A couple of music mates, including a true *trustafarian,* were the first wealthy dudes I'd befriended. I knew rich kids at Chapel Hill High School, like the guy with the party hippie parents. Their lives were so different from mine, I couldn't relate on a friendship level. I doubt anybody I'd worked with in the intervening years was wealthy. No sane wealthy person would choose the sort of grunt labor I did. Learning about the lives of the rich-if-not-famous from my buddies was interesting, but emphasized poverty's effect on my life. Poverty is truly an all-encompassing influence on multiple risks.

My first band might've sucked musically, but we had crowd appeal, so we made money. Shit-faced college crowds screamed as we banged out originals and covers in clubs, bars, and frat parties. I slowly integrated into the excellent Chapel Hill music scene. There were some great players in the area and jamming with them provided a rapid learning experience. The intense drug scene hadn't changed since my State days in Raleigh. A couple of the fine musicians I jammed with subsequently died of heroin overdoses.

I played music three or four nights a week and labored during the day. I had shoulder-length hair and was rail thin due to overwork and an impoverished diet, except for my Popeye forearms. The main health risk for a rock drummer who played in a lot of clubs and bars at the time was thick clouds of secondhand cigarette smoke. It was hard to rock out when I couldn't bloody breathe, and all my gear stunk of smoke. I was also lonely, a psychological risk. It surprised me when other drummers claimed they had no problems meeting women. Perhaps they were better drummers than me.

I found an urban surveying position. Surveying in the South was risky due to ungodly heat and humidity, snakes, ticks, hornets, bees, wasps, standing in the middle of roads, irate landowners, and so on. But poison ivy was the most irritating work risk.

I'd always been allergic to poison ivy, but I became more sensitized to it. Poison ivy is endemic in the South, especially along property lines and fences surveyors often have to follow. Summers were crushingly hot, so I wore as little clothing as possible, which didn't help. I became creative at urinating without touching my skin, but every year I suffered a rash where I wanted it least. This became critically important after I met Linda.

Despite my rocky lifestyle, Linda and I interlocked. A few things endeared her to me immediately, in no particular order: She liked my truck. She could drive the thing, which had power-nothing and a floor gear shift long enough to use as a hiking stick. Her excellent cooking. Our similar taste in movies. Her intelligence and humor. A personality that was the antithesis of my mother's. Her love of dogs. Her love of the outdoors, and our similar level of risk aversion in outdoor activities.

Linda was always independent, but she had entered a life-changing door when she spent three years as a teacher with the Peace Corps in western Kenya after her undergraduate education. Although most of the experience was positive, she encountered a few tense situations, including a riot at her school. A dictator ruled Kenya at the time. Her first real hiking trek was to the Langtang Valley in Nepal soon after she left the Peace Corps. The area is over twelve-thousand feet above sea level. I was impressed.

We moved in together shortly after we met, then married. There are severe risks associated with being unhappily married. These can be emotional, financial, and even physical in cases of domestic abuse. The risks can metastasize beyond partners to children, family, and friends. Linda and I haven't experienced such calamities. We've loved and respected each other for more than thirty years. I hope we have thirty more years together.

On our first camping trip, we bushwhacked to a remote section of Linville Gorge in the Appalachians. We wanted to camp undisturbed in an old-growth copse of giant tulip poplars, in autumn golden Lothlorien splendor. This began decades of mutual outdoor experiences. Linda trusts me as a risk manager, and I trust her. The relationship has been highly successful in wilderness experiences and all other aspects of life.

Our married lives have been far riskier in a voluntary sense compared to our single lives. There's a cliché about young people who lead "wild" lives. They're supposed to settle down and become more risk-averse when they age and become involved in long-term relationships. The cliché is laughable in our case, largely due to mountain climbing.

A major incident occurred early in our marriage which slammed shut my psychedelic experience door. In fact, it shut all the doors to illegal psychoactive substances. I practiced drums in our half of a duplex on—no joke—High Street, in Carrboro near Chapel Hill. Amazingly, our neighbors didn't object to the drums, despite the thin walls. At first, we lived next door to a couple of good ol' boys who often fought, but they'd bring women over and, from the sound of it, had exuberant group sex. Later, a nice young couple moved in. He strummed and sang tired old folk songs like "Kumbaya," and then they would have passionate, noisy sex. I was noisier, however.

A friend of Linda's once drove by the duplex and thought she heard thunder from a clear blue sky. Linda's explanation was, "Oh, that was just Robert practicing his drums." I whacked them hard in those days.

One afternoon I decided to trip while practicing. I'd obtained 'shrooms (Psilocybe cubensis) from a friend and ate a quarter ounce chopped up in honey to mask the taste. It was a large dose, but I'd routinely eaten that amount and more on previous trips. Things proceeded to get weird. I played along with Public Image Limited's *Album,* a brilliant but intensely negative rock recording, which probably didn't help. I found myself no longer playing the drum kit but banging my fists on a Granite Quarry granite coffee table, which was made from a rejected grave headstone. I'd smoked a lot of weed, and I found myself craving a beer. It was summer, and we didn't have air conditioning. I became increasingly agitated. No beer in the frig. I'm not sure it would've helped.

I started to have strange and violent thoughts, so I called Linda at work. She needed to ride her bike home, but during this time I worsened. I cycled through a large variety of sociopathic and psychopathic power trips in a rapid fashion, including those likely experienced by mass murderers and other power-mad individuals. I don't buy into the religious concept of evil, but this experience smacked me upside the head with the psychological concept.

Losing control of my mental processes, which had never happened before, was disturbing to say the least. I called 911 and pleaded, "I'm out of control, please come get me," and gave them the High Street address. They tried to get further information, but I spiraled into madness.

Linda, an ambulance, and the police all showed up at about the same time. Linda's coolness during this insane episode presaged her coolness in dangerous outdoor endeavors. I threw my half-naked body wildly around the room and tried to shoot laser beams out of my eyes at the emergency medical technicians (EMTs) and the cops.

The EMTs pulled Linda aside and asked, "Do you think he is acting a little strange?"

She exclaimed, "A *little?*"

I cycled between extreme agitation and slackness. The EMTs grabbed me while I slacked, strapped me to a gurney, and drove to the UNC ER. The stellate ambulance symbols surrounding the Rods of Asclepius on the back windows pulsated, as I repeated over and over, "It's an oscillating universe."

The ER felt like a nightmarish Pink Floyd video, or an abstract painting in motion, rendered by a mad god and populated by fuzzy demons. My glasses had been removed, which didn't help my perception. I knew I was in a hospital, but I couldn't see well.

It took five or six people to strap me down to a bed, and they weren't gentle. I would have killed them all without hesitation if I could've freed myself. The resident on call ordered naloxone, which did squat. Another medical error. It was highly unlikely I would've acted like this while on opiates or opioids, and naloxone counters the effects of these drugs. I told them repeatedly I had eaten psilocybin mushrooms. My psychotic behavior was admittedly not typical for psilocybin, either. Finally, they gave me the anti-psychotic drug haloperidol, which knocked me right out.

A blood test revealed the presence of a large amount of phentermine, a type of speed. The 'shrooms must have been soaked in it. The friend who sold them to me said they were strong, but he was unaware the dealer had soaked them in speed, probably to increase the bang per dose.

I never reacted well to speed, and I'd ingested a massive dose, combined with the psilocybin. According to anecdotal accounts on the Internet, most people find combinations of psychedelics and speed to be unpleasant at best.

After I regained some reason, a nurse came in to check on me. Unable to see well and thinking the woman was Linda, I tried to grab her leg, and she huffed, "Well, Mr. Lee, I think we're feeling a little better."

I was immensely grateful to retrieve my glasses, to be freed of restraints, and to finally see and hug the actual Linda.

It took me a while to recover from this extremely bad trip. The rewards associated with psychedelics had been profound, but I never wanted to descend through the hellish psychotic door again. I had no idea it would've been possible to experience such evil thoughts, or to lose complete control of my rationality. I detest being out of control.

While riding in the ambulance, I actively tried to die to escape the experience. As I was strapped down, and I couldn't convince my brain to shut down, I was unsuccessful. Such a mental state had never happened to me in well over one hundred psychedelic trips, over a period of ten years. A positive outcome might be a deeper understanding of how sociopaths and psychopaths think, but I could've done without any direct understanding.

I was pissed off afterward and tried to track down the jerk who spiked the 'shrooms. He got busted before I could get to him, probably good for both him and me. I might've had difficulty restraining myself.

I stopped taking psychedelics and using weed, cold turkey. I stopped using weed to avoid any sort of flashbacks. In retrospect, with more pharmaceutical knowledge, it was unlikely I would've returned to a psychotic state under the influence of cannabis, but I was unwilling to take the risk.

It took several months to psychologically deal with quitting weed. Cannabis isn't physically addictive like opioids, but I'd never experienced many aspects of adulthood without being stoned, particularly making love and playing rock music. Legal substances such as alcohol, caffeine, and sugar didn't substitute. It wasn't easy, but I got over it.

There were no legal repercussions from this psychotic episode. Perhaps the cops thought they hallucinated it. I never saw them again. I suffered no legal consequences from my illegal drug use at all. I was never busted, and to my knowledge neither were any of my friends. This was fortunate, as being arrested and convicted can have lifelong consequences.

∿

I was sick of working around poison ivy in the Southern heat, and saw no real future in either manual labor or full-time music. I looked for an employment alternative. I was fortunate, shortly after my psychotic event, to score a job in the same UNC toxicology and pharmacology lab where Linda worked.

They hired me because I had become, according to my surveying partner Hank's wise advice, smarter than the equipment. The lab housed a graveyard of liquid and gas chromatographs, proto-personal computers, and other complex equipment; dead until I got there and fixed them. I also learned practical skills associated with pharmacology research.

Rat and mouse bites were a risk in this lab, as the rodents objected to being tortured and decapitated in the name of science. The drugs shot into their brains in experiments were often labeled with radioactive compounds. A lot of radioactivity floated about, as some lab users, especially medical students, weren't as careful as they should've been with the compounds. The entire lab required periodic decontamination as a result.

It was my first job involving toxicology and radioactivity, which interested me and proved to be important in my eventual career.

When I told my co-worker and friend Tim I was leaving surveying, he lamented, "Why you want to go work with a bunch of nerds?" Tim was a unique character who played guitar in a hair-metal band. His idea of humor was to expel a silent-but-deadly in the work truck and then roll up the windows in a quietly casual manner. He'd laughed uproariously when he heard about my psychotic episode, visualizing me running down High Street half-naked and brandishing a machete.

I, too, have questioned my career decision over the years. Despite my youthful nerd-branding, I had little in common with many scientists. My good ol' boy youth and young adulthood may have hampered my scientific career path. I neither know nor do I care. I also don't regret abandoning back work for brain work. It gave me more freedom, and it paid more. However, I'm glad I had direct experience and understanding of the poor side of the economic door.

The "poor side" of the economic door is relative, of course. Linda and I decided to visit Kenya shortly after we married. Linda's Peace Corps experience had affected her to a substantial degree, and she wanted to share it with me. I'd never been outside North America and it sounded interesting.

The sights, sounds, and smells of East Africa were a big smack upside my American head. The trip was difficult because we had little money and the plane fare was expensive. Instead of doing organized tourist things like safaris and staying in nice hotels, we traveled on the cheap and camped most of the time.

Aside from Linda's experience and contacts, we lacked good *beta* (a climbing term for useful information) for the trip, and some activities were rather risky. Linda was accustomed to some of these risks, but I wasn't. They provide a good illustration of how risk perception can differ depending on how familiar a person is with a particular situation.

For example, rather than touring around in posh Land Rovers, we took public transportation. This involved *matatus*, small pickup trucks crammed with people and livestock, overloaded buses, and worst of all, Peugeot *flying coffins*. These were station wagons capable of high speeds, often crashing and killing the occupants. It was tense. We were close to getting robbed a couple of times. Check points were manned by AK-47 wielding police demanding bribes from drivers. They'd give us the eye, but let us pass, probably because we obviously had little money.

We didn't visit the most famous game parks. Predators such as lions will hunt humans who are on foot, and we couldn't afford to go on a vehicle safari. So, we hiked through Hell's Gate National Park, which had no lions.

While walking a bushy trail we came around a corner and encountered some dudes in fatigues with AK-47s. I was apprehensive, but Linda pointed out the little rhino pins on their berets and assured me they were game wardens. They had the authority to shoot poachers on sight. We obviously weren't poachers. They chatted with us in the cross-tribal language Swahili, then invited us to their dry shack to quaff warm Cokes. Some young Maasai dudes showed up in full traditional garb and weaponry. We couldn't communicate much, but it was a cool encounter.

In a forested area of the park, while looking up and observing a barrel of monkeys in the trees, I stepped on a column of safari ants. They safaried up my leg and I received a few painful bites. This prompted me to carry a can of "It," or DDT-in-a-spray-can.

While taking photos of a troop of baboons, the large alpha male strutted out front and displayed vivid gestures and an angry demeanor, suggesting he intended to rip my ass to shreds if I got any closer. I respected his wishes and backed off slowly and submissively. I was accustomed to baboonish behavior from my tree-planting days.

❧

Mt. Elgon is a 14,000-plus foot extinct shield volcano of huge areal extent, similar to the Hawaiian Big Island, on the Kenyan and Ugandan border. We decided to make an ascent, which typically takes several days of hiking. Ugandan cattle rustlers sometimes raided the Kenyans, and then escaped back over the mountain. The local forestry office revealed they had run the rustlers armed with AKs out of mountain-town, which was reassuring.

It was a fascinating trek that ascended through several distinct ecosystems, including bamboo forest, cloud forest, and eventually tropical alpine meadows dotted with giant groundsels, lobelias, and other uniquely weird plants.

In the bamboo forest zone, we picked a nice flat campsite after sunset. The next morning, we saw why our campsite was nice and flat; it was in the middle of an elephant trail. Good thing the elephants hadn't taken an evening stroll.

Linda and I slept in an old stone hut above timberline for a couple of nights. Rustlers had broken off the wooden door and burned most of it for heat. One night, hyenas snuffled around the open doorway, which I'd tried to block with remaining pieces of wood. I kept a pile of substantial rocks by my sleeping bag and threw them at the interlopers all bloody night long. I was prepared to use my trusty *panga* (machete) if throwing rocks didn't work. We didn't need no stinkin' door to keep animals at bay. Despite a sleepless night, we enjoyed magical views from the summit, and witnessed a rare snowfall on the equatorial mountain.

We then decided to explore the substantial Cherangani Hills, the tallest over 11,000 feet. I'm not sure what prompted this decision; maybe just an interesting blank spot on the tourist map we carried.

We didn't have detailed maps or any useful beta. At one time, the British produced a series of excellent topographic maps of the country, but they had been confiscated by the Kenyans for "security" reasons. Additionally, there were reports of tribal conflicts over grazing lands. No worries. As far as I could tell from our crude map, which represented the approximately thirty by thirty-mile Hills area by a little patch an inch in diameter, we could traverse the Hills and end up in the Rift Valley, and catch a bus back to a town on what appeared to be a tarmac road. I estimated the trek would take us three or four days. We stocked up on canned goods and the like, as lightweight camping food wasn't found in Kenya at the time.

Unfortunately, no trail system *per se* existed. Paths connected small *shambas* (farming homesteads) and didn't follow a logical route to traverse the range. There was little reason for the locals to do so, as they were largely self-sufficient farmers. Although Linda knew the basics of Swahili, most of the local people didn't speak it, so it was difficult to get any sort of beta. We didn't want to bother or encounter people, anyway. We were only interested in hiking.

After many miles of wandering around the countryside we attained a wide trail, or old road, on a ridge in the center of the range. A local, a young man much larger than me who strangely knew a few words of English, demanded our shoes, our gear, and so on. I noted a group of men stalking us on the trail from the other direction. It seemed a little dicey. We were armed with one panga, which happened to be out of reach on my pack.

I whispered, "Linda, hand me the panga," but she thought this might escalate matters, a reasonable assumption. We were on our own in a remote corner of a deeply foreign land.

So, with a, "See ya!" to the giant kid, we bailed off the trail into a wilderness stream valley paralleling the ridge. I assumed there would be a trail by the stream. As it turned out, there was good reason nobody followed us.

Bushwhacking in this area of Kenya wasn't pleasant, due to thick, thorny, and noxious-sapped undergrowth. No doubt venomous snakes were present as well, although we didn't encounter any. Linda wore a culturally appropriate long skirt, not anticipating thorny bushwhacking. Her legs in particular were vegetatively flayed, but all uncovered parts of our bodies were bloodied. I, at least, wore long pants.

After a mile or so of medieval-esque torture, we reached the stream which ran through lovely virgin tropical forest, but still no trail. We discussed our predicament in a lively fashion. I noticed a local man, dressed in a loincloth and carrying a bow, arrows and a spear, on the other side of the stream. He probably belonged to the indigenous Sengwer tribe. He pointed to the ground repeatedly with his spear and then disappeared. Linda and I crossed the stream and found a trail on the other side. Cheers, brother!

We encountered an unexpected situation one night when I couldn't build a campfire. We carried a butane stove for cooking. I'd built fires at other camps on this jaunt, theoretically for keeping animals at bay. I thought I could build a fire anywhere, due to my extensive sodden experiences in the woods. The camp was among an unusual grove of trees, possibly a species of Schefflera similar to a common houseplant. The weather was fine, the copious dead wood perfectly dry, but it simply wouldn't burn. I even held twigs over the butane stove; they just charred and never burst into flame. The trees were also small and twisted. We reckoned why this nice grove of trees still existed while much of the surrounding land had been cleared for farms: the wood was useless for anything, so the trees were spared. I piled a bunch of rocks by the tent door and kept the panga close at hand for animal defense. Thankfully, we had no adverse encounters.

In this and other areas of the Cherangani Hills, we frightened children who'd never seen *mzungus* (Whites) before. Indeed, I'm fairly confident this was the first time mzungus had traversed this route, as the Hills were never colonized by the Brits, and this area was way off the beaten tourist track.

As we approached the far side of the Hills, kind locals indicated that the last remaining ridge before attaining the Rift Valley proper was inhabited by people who wouldn't take kindly to mzungus. They pointed to us, to the ridge, and made getting-shot-with-an-arrow and stabbing motions. Not wanting to aggravate or fend off such folk with a single panga, we decided to descend into a stream valley in a torrential downpour, where there appeared to be a small village.

We came upon an abandoned stone house with an intact metal roof in an area where the locals lived in mud huts with thatch roofing. The structure had historically housed White missionaries. The locals we talked to weren't interested in it. It was unclear whether this was because of the style or some bad mojo. However, every invertebrate from miles around loved it because they could escape from the rain. The floor literally moved with large ants, beetles, and other creatures; it was like a scene in an Indiana Jones movie. I retrieved my trusty can of It and dispersed the residents. The risk of DDT exposure mattered little to us under the circumstances.

The next day we hiked out, eventually attaining a dirt road and a small store at the edge of the Rift Valley. We guzzled warm Cokes and choked down soda crackers.

It took us a total of six days to cross the range. The traverse took longer than anticipated, and for the only time in our many wilderness experiences, we ran out of food. If we'd been desperate, though, we probably could've hit up the locals for vegetables or a chicken. I seriously doubt anybody else has been silly enough to repeat this trek.

The only adverse consequence of the Kenya trip was Linda contracting a bad case of campylobacteriosis. We were careful in food preparation, boiling water, personal hygiene, and so on, but it's difficult for the immune systems of most North Americans to deal with the plethora of infection risks in a country such as Kenya. It's a major reason we're not interested in extensive international travel.

After several years in Chapel Hill, we were both eager to escape the South and the East in general. Linda wanted to become an epidemiologist, subsequent to her Peace Corps experience. Several graduate schools accepted her, including the University of Washington. I voted for this option and was hired over the phone by a Principal Investigator who learned I could fix laboratory equipment. Being smarter than the equipment proved, once again, to be a useful attribute.

Moving to Washington provided the opportunity to climb through a series of mountainous risk doors.

Ma and Pa Cook and Lee in the Cherangani Hills, Kenya. "Like to pack heavy, dontcha son?" (credit: R. C. Lee).

The Cascade Door

WE HIKE TO THE BLINDING LOWER SNOWFIELDS ON MT. BAKER AND CAMP. We see a passel of mountain club members camping higher up, and Paul suggests, "We'll get up early." Early indeed. We trudge roped across the crevassed glacier in the early morning glow. Paul and I arrive at the base of the North Ridge ahead of the other groups. The route is glacier ice and steep snow climbing, up to a seventy-degree angle, for about 3,000 feet. I've never climbed anything like this in my life, but I reckon Paul knows what he's doing. I'm armed with a crappy, long handled ice ax and a shorter ice hammer, flexible leather boots, and crappy dull crampons. I launch off on my first alpine ice climb; indeed my first substantial roped climb. At the steepest pitch Paul hands me a bunch of dull, old-school ice screws and offers, "Go ahead, you lead." I express some reservations, but he replies, "Just put in the pro, you'll be fine." I hack away at the ice, releasing large, dinner plate-size hunks down onto the heads of the club members, who inexplicably cluster at the base of the pitch below me. I struggle to place the dull screws, but the ice is forgiving. Summiting takes longer than if I knew what I was doing, but I discover technical climbing speaks loudly to me. I climb through the door to the real mountains.

Linda and I relocated to Seattle in a four-cylinder, two-seater, Mazda pickup truck, which strained to pull a U-Haul filled with our few possessions. Falling asleep at the wheel concerned us. The vehicle only had a radio, and since neither of us are fans of country music, we suffered with no musical stimulation through much of the heartland. The gas station coffee we tried to choke down tasted like brewed cigarette butts, so we lacked chemical stimulation as well. Despite drowsy driving, we arrived without incident.

We initially rented a house from a demented woman who moved into the basement while we occupied the upper floor. She became increasingly paranoid and accused me of shooting laser beams late at night. This wasn't an unreasonable accusation, if she had seen me on High Street. The rental situation didn't last long. We moved into a dank, moldy duplex, and later bought our first house.

It's hard to imagine we spent ten years in rainy Seattle, especially in light of my previous sodden experiences in Alaska and the Pacific Northwest, and the fact that I now have seasonal affective disorder. The rise of gourmet coffee during the late 1980s and early 1990s helped. I also knew Washington had lots of mountains; I just had to wait for them.

Seattle was the epicenter of the *grunge* music quake. I auditioned with a few bands, but I needed to decide whether to bet on a musical career or stay in science. It was difficult to relate to other rock musicians without indulging in drugs. Plus, I'd cut my hair, and I suffered back issues from playing rock drums with poor form.

I also tried playing percussion with some excellent New Age musicians. New Age was a less physically demanding and drug-ridden musical form prevalent in Seattle at the time, but the genre didn't speak to me. Linda described it as "after-school-special music." A percussionist playing these soothing tunes risked narcolepsy. Nonetheless, a band offered me a spot on a several-month European tour, a rather big break for an aspiring professional musician.

Betting on a musical career crossed a financial risk red line, however, and I was unwilling to leave Linda for so long. Music went by the wayside for more than ten years, while I focused on work, graduate school, and mountains.

We didn't start technical mountain climbing right away. We attempted alpine or downhill skiing at lift-served ski areas. We'd both done some cross-country skiing, and I had my useless Hoodsie Woodsie experience, but great rewards seemed to be associated with alpine skiing. There had to be a good reason crowds of people from toddlers to geezers enjoyed it and spent large amounts of time and money doing it. Entire mountain towns have been built around skiing. Economists call this phenomenon *willingness-to-pay* for a reward.

We were more interested in ski mountaineering, or climbing mountains and skiing back down, but first we needed to learn to turn. A local shopping mall housed a ridiculous angled rolling carpet contraption in which the carpet rolled upward, and we could sort of slalom back and forth across it. They even provided skis. We carpet-skied a couple of times and were ready for the slopes.

We had no money for gear, lessons, or lift tickets at a proper resort. We rented skis and boots, and visited the cheapest, lift-served area near Seattle at the low-elevation Snoqualmie Pass. It sometimes snowed there, but mostly it rained during the day and froze at night. Skiing at night cost even less.

Driving to the slopes at night could be an adventure. I'd load sandbags and chains into the rear-wheel-drive Mazda and hope the plows had done their jobs. Installing chains in the dark with freezing hands while mucking around in mud and slush seriously sucked. Driving back to town at night sucked worse. The worst drivers appeared to be those with 4WD vehicles. They seemed to think 4WD made them invincible, even when they applied brakes on ice while speeding downhill.

Using our carpet-skiing skills, we valiantly tried to snowplow down sheets of ice. The carpet training was useless. We mostly just slid down the hill on our bodies rather than on our skis. I don't think I've ever been so embarrassed. I once caught a ski tip on something while loading on the lift and fell off the chair, much to the other skiers' amusement. In a loud and derisive fashion, other skiers introduced us to the term *yard sale*, a situation in which one's released skis and poles are scattered across a slope after a bad fall.

We were bruised all over but felt fortunate we didn't break anything. We probably suffered ligament and spinal disc damage. Nobody wore helmets, for which I have no explanation, aside from their relative heaviness back then. Such a learning experience would be bad enough for children, but it was downright painful and humiliating for two large, healthy adults.

We persevered though, and later our friend Ultra-Dan took us under his wing and taught us a little. We called him Ultra-Dan because he excelled at whatever athletic activity he undertook. One spring we met him at Mt. St. Helens, where he'd just telemarked down the 4,000 feet of snow on skinny cross-country skis and leather boots, and was heading up with a snowboard to descend again. He could pinhead well, and this was before snowboarding was even a thing.

Dan had an aggressive teaching style. For example, he took me to the top of a steep Stevens Pass ski run named Double Diamond. It looked nearly vertical to a newbie skier. He encouraged me to make one turn at a time in two feet of fresh, gloppy snow, and then to try two linked turns, all the way down the long run. His patience was boundless.

Somehow, Linda and I learned enough to start skiing down mountains. It felt like a literal school of hard knocks. We saved money and bought cheap ski-mountaineering rigs. We affectionately called the crappy skis *chatter boards,* because they vibrated uncontrollably on hard snow. Nonetheless, we skied many mountains, including the volcanoes Mt. St. Helens and Mt. Adams, with these lame rigs.

Then there was climbing. Linda and I scrambled up some easy peaks, but technical climbing started in earnest once we met Paul. He was a physician who'd climbed hundreds of peaks, rock routes, and canyoneering routes all over the world. At a university picnic I attended with Linda, I wore a shirt printed with Puebloan-inspired petroglyph figures, as well as flying saucers, coffee cups, and other silly, fake petroglyph-ish figures.

Paul approached and asked seriously, "I see you like petroglyphs; do you enjoy canyoneering?" It was then that he noticed the flying saucers, but my shirt had started a conversation about the outdoors.

I told him about my Paria experience, leaving out Bill the Cat, and mentioned I'd done some rock climbing and easy mountaineering. Unbeknown to me, Paul had previously approached the local mountain club when he moved to Seattle and presented his extensive and impressive resume. Much to his irritation, the club wouldn't let him join a mountaineering trip until he'd gone through their training process. He therefore roped me into my first substantial technical alpine climb.

I led part of the North Ridge of Mt. Baker. The majority of climbing risk is borne by the leader, on *the sharp end* of the rope. A fall in lead position can be much further compared to the second climber, who's roped from above. The ice pro at the time, shitty screws, was often psychological at best and probably wouldn't have held a substantial fall. So, my years of soloing on rock proved useful. It's never a good idea to fall on ice anyway.

Ice climbers wear sharp objects on their feet and carry them in their hands. I'm not sure why Paul trusted me to lead, but it all worked out fine.

We enjoyed many subsequent years of climbing and skiing adventures. Paul was a highly intelligent physician, and had a cornucopia of interesting ER and climbing stories. He punctuated his written trip reports with pithy statements such as "Boring," "Fun!" and, "We almost died," sometimes all on the same page. If anybody complained, he'd always say, "Would you like some cheese with your whine?"

He had an unusually objective view of risk, which may have influenced my own view. For example, when we started out driving from Seattle, he often advised, "Okay, Robert, this is the most dangerous part of the climb." In a statistical sense this was true. Many climbers and skiers think because they're good at their sports they can also drive well, which may or may not be the case. Even if they're skilled drivers, other drivers may not be, and other mountain driving risks exist such as collisions with wildlife. However, the comparative risk between driving and climbing depends on the type of climbing. Sport climbing, for example, is a popular type of modern rock climbing using pre-existing steel expansion bolt anchors as pro on short, solid rock pitches. It's quite safe compared to, say, difficult waterfall ice climbing in remote areas, or high-altitude mountaineering.

The next climb with Paul was also a new experience for me. Mt. Triumph is an aesthetic rock peak in the North Cascades involving a long hike, a glacier crossing, and a large technical rock pyramid featuring the classic Northeast Ridge. I'd never placed rock protection on lead before. Paul brought a big rack of nuts and an early incarnation of cams for pro. I led some *pitches* (rope lengths) near my soloing limit on a remote peak, while at the same time, figuring out how to use the pro. I remembered to be smarter than the equipment.

Then came time to descend. It was a long route, and Paul brought two one-hundred-and-sixty-foot (fifty-meter) ropes, typical practice at the time. It took forever to rap down the route. It was my first substantial rapping. I'd done some previous short raps using the old *Dulfersitz* method, which is clumsy and painful. It requires wrapping the rope around your body for friction instead of using a device attached to your harness. I was finally bounding outwards with a rap device.

Rapping is quite safe if everything is set up correctly and the anchor is *bomber* (solid and reliable). If not, rapping is one of the riskiest aspects of roped climbing. If the anchor fails, the climber goes splat. These days, climbers would probably carry two thin, two-hundred-foot (sixty-meter) ropes if they planned to rap such a route. They could descend further in a single go. Regardless, we made it back to our camp before dark, always a worthy goal.

As we packed up the next day, I leaned over and gouged my forehead on my pack-mounted ice ax. It bled profusely. I asked Paul if I could borrow his first aid kit. Mine was in the bottom of my pack.

"I have surgical tape and Percocet. If you need more than that, you need a helicopter."

I thought this seemed oddly minimalistic at the time, but he was correct in most situations. I stuck a piece of tape on my forehead and we hiked out.

Paul hooked me, and subsequently Linda, on technical mountaineering, and was a fine mentor. We roped ourselves through the technical climbing door.

I'd previously thought ropework, placing protection, and other hall-marks of roped climbing were arcane and complex, and I'd little desire to learn. I came to realize roped climbing was simple if I was smarter than the equipment and stayed focused. Using ropes allowed me to travel in a wide range of terrain in safety, or at least in safety compared to being un-roped. I also learned wearing rock shoes with sticky rubber soles made harder rock climbing a helluva lot easier and safer than wearing boots.

Mountaineering: The Freedom of the Hills, published by The Mountaineers, is a well-known mountaineering instructional text. The book wasn't particularly useful to me, but the concept of *the freedom of the hills* reso-nated. I wanted to be able to go wherever I wanted in the hills and wilder-ness, within the constraints of risk and physical ability. Later, Linda joined me in my quest. We found the freedom-of-the-hillbilly path to be worthy of great effort and attention. In this case, Homer's reflection "the journey is the thing" was bang-on.

I found the rewards of more intense wilderness experiences equivalent to a stoned state in many ways. I'd discovered a cognitive substitute more addictive than the drugs I'd taken for years. I'm unsure why harder climbing was so addictive. Perhaps it was because such climbing was a more intense version of what I already loved; immersed in wild environments, managing risk so I could climb again and again without dying.

I didn't document climbs until many years later when I was laid up from a climbing accident and had time to go through guidebooks. Paul, in contrast, kept a detailed, annotated log and, later on, spreadsheets of all his climbs. I was simply never peak-goal oriented, in contrast to the simple goal of traveling in cool wilderness.

Most climbers are goal-oriented, and more successful than Linda and me in terms of the number of peaks or routes, or difficulty of routes, within a particular span of time. Paul was an example. Many climbers also set goals such as climbing new routes or unclimbed peaks, attaining a certain level of difficulty, and climbing all the peaks over a particular elevation. Many top-tier climbers also want to try and make a living at it, in order to climb on a continuous basis. Some become sponsored professional climbers or mountain guides. Others become pro mountain photographers or writers.

Good for them. Linda and I weren't interested. By the time we started technical climbing together, we considered having good human relationships, interesting and productive scientific careers, and enjoying a life beyond climbing more important. We were also more interested in being in wilderness than on top of peaks, but there are lots of wilderness peaks.

As we became experts in roped climbing, we visited many places rarely or ever touched by humans. We climbed hundreds of technical routes and peaks over a quarter century. Our criteria were simple: routes and peaks had to be high quality, aesthetically pleasing, within our physical capabilities, and in places we could experience by ourselves. We were indeed alone in the vast majority of cases. We were even alone on popular peaks by climbing them in mid-week, or in winter.

There were only a few routes we didn't complete once we decided to climb them, largely because we just didn't want to go back. In the Cascades, sometimes it took a couple of attempts, usually due to rain. Snow was fine, but approaching, camping, and climbing in the rain were miserable unless we had no choice, like in Scotland. Repeating climbs didn't interest us unless, for example, we wanted to do a winter ascent after having made a summer ascent.

When they discuss trips they've made, climbers often focus on the ones which were particularly dangerous or where things went wrong, as they make more compelling stories. The mountaineering literature reflects this. The climbs described here imparted important risk lessons. However, the majority of climbs we completed were relatively uneventful, so I don't want to convey the impression that our lives were constantly threatened.

Climbing with a partner or partners introduces the concept of managing risks for yourself and others, on a continuous basis. In roped climbing, a climber is literally tied to their partner. I tried to limit partners to those who were fit, competent, funny, and didn't freak out. But the *brotherhood of the rope* goes beyond those attributes. It demands an ethical and moral commitment to your partners.

Telling yourself, "Badass Dude climbed Heinous Route on Gnarly Peak, so he must be a great partner," is a risky presumption. Nothing could be further from the truth. I've known great climbers who climbed much harder routes than I ever did, yet I didn't find them thoughtful risk managers and therefore would never get close to a mountain with them.

The moral dilemmas associated with climbing with partners good and bad are explored in many classic works of mountaineering literature. The fine memoir and subsequent documentary *Touching the Void* by Joe Simpson is perhaps the most eloquent. In this extreme scenario, a climber cut the rope to his partner hanging below, to avoid sliding down the mountain and dying himself. He reckoned there was a good chance his partner had died, but wasn't certain. He felt as though he had no other options.

It was more complicated than this, with much heartfelt soul-searching. The author was the partner hanging below, so—spoiler alert—he didn't die. He describes the moral dilemma and the tradeoffs much better than I can here. Few climbers will ever find themselves in this situation, severing the brotherhood-of-the-rope for the sake of their own survival. The answers still surprised me when I posed an informal survey question on a climbing Internet forum, soon after the documentary came out: "Would you have cut the rope?" Several dozen respondents all claimed they would've cut in this situation. I then knew who to avoid as partners, or at least make sure they didn't have a knife handy.

My moral tie to Linda is much stronger than to some random dude, who may be fit, competent, un-freakable, and a fine funny fellow, otherwise. I would never have cut a rope attached to Linda had there been the slightest chance she was alive. I would've suffered severe clinical depression or worse had I made such a decision. My bond with Linda was too much to ask of other partners, as I wasn't married to them. Many people simply won't compromise their own survival for somebody else.

Some respondents to the survey even expressed agitation. "Who the hell are you? You aren't a badass climbing routes like those guys, so what do you know?" This wasn't a coherent argument. Climbers don't have to be members of the badass tribe to encounter dangerous situations and manage risk as a good climbing partner. My life is evidence of that.

In the popular imagination, fear is associated with climbing. Some accomplished climbers claim they often feel the strong emotion of fear. In contrast, Linda once observed, "You can't be a climber if you're afraid of dying." Many seem to be afraid, however.

I've felt anger, sadness, joy, and other emotions while climbing, but never fear. Neither has Linda. Maybe different people define fear in different ways. Some climbers speak of conquering their fear, or similar sentiments. This confuses me, and I ask the question: "Then why the hell do you keep climbing?" It seems mighty risky to me to be conquering strong emotions during a difficult climb, rather than focusing on the task at hand.

Linda and I wouldn't have continued technical climbing if we'd felt fear. She consistently kept her focus and a cool, rational head. She never expressed a desire to back off a climb I didn't back off from first. We were similar in our attitudes toward risk, never freaked out, made good mutual decisions in the mountains, climbed a lot of them, and always made it home alive, still married. I couldn't have asked for a better partner. The only things that freak Linda out are tiny arachnids.

Being a member of a tribe of supportive edgeworkers can be a mechanism for fear management. Climbers are a distinct tribe among outdoor athletes. However, I rarely felt like I was part of a climbing community or tribe, except perhaps later, in the bizarre specialties of waterfall ice and mixed ice and rock climbing. My lack of tribal affinity may have been due to climbing solo for so long before I started roped climbing, or the fact that I started roped climbing so late in life. Once Linda started climbing, we largely just climbed with each other. If I couldn't find a good partner otherwise, I'd solo. I never viewed climbing as a social scene, and I found I'd little in common with many climbers.

Additionally, clubby recreational climbing can be risky. Clustering at the base of an ice climb on Mt. Baker and getting pummeled with icy dinner-plates, for example, could have been fatal. We met exceptional Cascades climbers, such as Fred Beckey, Jim Nelson, and the Skoog brothers, but we found the club culture stifling.

Linda and I joined the local Seattle club to learn which climbs to avoid on particular weekends. They emphasized large groups, which slowed their climbs to a glacial pace, thereby increasing risk. Time is the climber's enemy. The longer climbers are in the mountains, the longer they're vulnerable to risk, but the club didn't seem to understand this. Large groups also increased the probability of rockfall, human error, and other risks.

We witnessed groups of roped-up club members sporting long, old-school ice axes and carrying large packs containing camping equipment on easy rock scrambles, even though there was no snow and they weren't camping. They also seemed to be years behind the times in terms of technology. For example, they didn't allow *belay* (a method of securing and feeding out and taking in rope) and rap devices for years after they were accepted everywhere else. The club also contributed to *soft* ratings which exaggerated the difficulty for Cascade climbs. When we climbed elsewhere, we were often taken aback by how difficult, say, a 5.8 rated rock climb was outside of the Cascades.

The club also seemed oblivious to the existence of mountain professionals, although there weren't many in the US at the time. Later, when I hired and befriended pro mountain guides in Canada, I found their expertise invaluable for learning how to climb efficiently and safely alone, and with Linda and other partners. Previous mentors like Paul helped, but certified mountain guides are a higher form of risk-management-life. Not all guides, however, are cool cats. This is reflected in the old joke:

"What's the difference between God and a mountain guide?"

"God doesn't think he's a mountain guide."

Most of the guides I climbed with were indeed cool cats. Guides also facilitate rewarding mountain experiences for others, which goes beyond the selfish act of climbing itself.

Paul turned me on to the classic book *Climbing Ice,* by the great climber and billionaire Yvon Chouinard. The book influenced my climbing style and intrigued me with its photos of alpine and waterfall ice climbing. Chouinard's philosophy was *fast and light is right.* He admonished climbers to carry as little as possible for the sake of speed, and to leave many of the recommended *Ten Essentials* at home. He suggested that carrying *bivi* gear (bivouac, or camping gear) caused them to bivi regardless of whether they planned this or not, due to their slow pace while carrying heavy loads. Apostate! I thought it was great advice. European climbing culture influenced Chouinard to a great degree. Those folks have been climbing hard for more than a hundred years.

Linda's and my eyes were opened to Euro-style when we first climbed in the French and Italian Alps, after she completed a work-related trip in Lyon. The Chamonix and Courmayeur area is one of the world centers for people who do risky stuff in the mountains. The number of routes and the number of people climbing them are mind-blowing. Many of the routes, even the easier classics, are highly exposed and dangerous due to both natural and human factors.

The entire scene differed from the Cascades. Instead of expeditions plodding along with big packs and grim demeanors, brightly colored, spandex-encased, skinny-assed men and women practically skipped up the things, and then flew off with parasails. It seemed crazy at the time, but later I appreciated the Alpen Climber Way: climb as fast as possible, get off the mountain, and back to the hut or town to eat good food, drink wine, and make love. The area also has world-class professional rescue services and dozens of mountain guides if climbers get into trouble, which was new to us.

Another shock was the size of the big routes on Mt. Blanc, which are Alaskan in scale. A mountain guide friend once described a potential client's mindset as "his eyes are bigger than his stomach." Technical routes such as the Brenva and Peuterey Ridges, the latter being one of the longest routes in the Alps, looked compelling in the photos and guidebooks, and ass-puckering viewed in person. However, we were there early in the season, and there'd been a substantial new snowfall. Nobody was climbing on Mt. Blanc due to avalanche risk.

We were limited to climbing more moderate objectives, which was fortunate. We weren't fast enough at the time to climb such massive routes in good time. Perhaps we could've climbed these routes years later, but we never went back. There were too many mountains in the world.

Risk is not necessarily determined by a climb's size or technical difficulty, and I experienced many risky moments in the Cascades. For example, long bushwhacking approaches in the North Cascades were often merely unpleasant, but getting injured or lost in the process were real possibilities. The approaches to some climbs were arguably more difficult than the climbs themselves. This was the case when Paul, our friend Ron, and I climbed Mt. Fury as well as the Price Glacier on Mt. Shuksan in the North Cascades. The climbs were almost a relief after the horrific bushy off-trail approaches.

Cascades weather was a dominant issue any time of year. Paul and I ascended the Muir Snowfield on Mt. Rainier in midwinter, with the intention of skiing 4,000 feet down from the Muir Hut to the parking lot. It went fine, other than the clouds rose as we descended, and we found ourselves trying to ski in a total *whiteout*, with no geographic points of reference. Skiing in a whiteout is like skiing inside of a ping-pong ball in high wind. At times, I couldn't even tell whether I was moving or not. It was nauseating.

We were concerned about losing daylight, as we were traveling fast-and-light and didn't have bivi gear. Not showing up that evening in Seattle would've been rather embarrassing, not to mention precipitating a rescue. This was before cell phones. We knew if we skied too far to the right, we ran the risk of skiing off massive cliffs down to the Nisqually Glacier and breaking our bodies into little pieces. On the other hand, we knew if we skied too far to the left, we'd run into the road or a broad ridge. We erred on the side of safety and made it home that night. Erring on the side of certainty or safety is a basic mountain navigation technique.

Whiteout conditions are dangerous because the skier is moving fast and trying to slide downhill under control, while trying to avoid flying off a cliff or into a crevasse. The Cascades taught me to ski-by-feel. My previous surveying experience was superb navigation training as well. Many people today use GPS, but frankly, if mountain travelers have to rely on GPS for navigation, they aren't thinking like risk managers. Electronic devices or batteries can fail.

Avalanches are an uncontrollable risk unless a mountain traveler simply stays out of avalanche terrain, or the snow has been released using explosives. Climbers and skiers can manage when they go, where they go, and how they go, but in avalanche terrain during high-risk periods, it's a roll of the dice. Avalanches are similar to earthquakes; they can be highly destructive, and unpredictable to a large degree. Transceivers or other devices used to locate buried victims are poor substitutes for avoiding avalanches to begin with. The Cascade snowpack is often predictable compared to many ranges, but the unexpected can still occur.

Linda, Ron and I climbed the Coleman Headwall on Mt. Baker, ascending 2,500 feet of steep snow and ice. This is a riskier route than the North Ridge. It's longer and holds more snow, and large avalanches can occur. We camped on the glacier below. The next morning, we climbed the lower wall in darkness. We *simul-climbed* or climbed while simultaneously roped, but not belayed. This is standard practice on glaciers. If one partner falls into a hidden crevasse covered by snow the others can theoretically stop the fall and rescue him. We didn't think, however, about the implications of simul-climbing on the steep snow and ice wall without setting *running pro* (protection clipped to the rope, without belaying) between the partners.

At the time, unprotected simul-climbing was standard practice on Cascade faces and ridges. Most climbers just stayed roped up and moved together without pro. If the route was steep and one partner fell, the other members were supposed to self-arrest, but unless they did it quickly and correctly, everyone tumbled down. This practice wasn't limited to the Cascades. On popular snow faces in the Alps for example, *flossing* occurred when the roped party wiped off other parties below when they fell. Yep, this has happened. I hope the practice has changed.

Linda and I wouldn't have climbed in this fashion after gaining more experience. Rather, we would have un-roped, placed running pro, or belayed to stop a fall. Carrying enough *snow pickets* (long pieces of channeled aluminum hammered into the snow) and ice screws to protect this route would've made a heavy load. It was probably best to have climbed unroped. With two ice tools and crampons, climbers are self-belayed. They just have to stick to the mountain and not lose it.

We climbed the route in good time regardless, descended the *dog* (easy or tourist) route, and were back at our tents by early afternoon. As we were relaxing, a large avalanche wiped almost the entire face. This was started by *serac* fall, a glacial ice cliff or big hunk of ice giving way. If we'd been on the face at the time, we would've certainly died. We weren't carrying transceivers, but it wouldn't have made any difference.

Avalanches are a dominant concern when backcountry skiing or ski mountaineering. In the Cascades, the snow often stabilizes quickly after a storm, and a skier can be somewhat confident it isn't going to release on him. In the spring, *corn* snow forms, which is easy to ski and usually stable. Linda and I skied the volcanoes Mt. St. Helens and Mt. Adams, for example, in corn conditions. In ranges such as the Canadian and much of the American Rockies, buried, weakened layers can persist all winter, and it's often a crap shoot as to whether a particular slope will release or not as a skier descends.

We never did much hard-core wilderness skiing, largely because it took so long for us to become good at it. There's an orders-of-magnitude difference between cross-country skiing on a nice rolling trail and descending a two-thousand-foot, forty-degree chute down a big mountain, safely and efficiently. A skier needs to be damn confident to ski such lines. Falling can lead to serious injury or death. It's just never a good idea to fall anyway, even at a resort.

Additionally, skiers don't have the safety of a rope, glacier skiing being an exception. They're entirely dependent on their ability to turn to control speed, change direction, and stop, while their feet are clamped to long slippery boards. It took us a couple of decades to get to the point where we can ski most conditions with confidence, or at least get down without dying. I rarely smiled with pleasure while climbing, but I often smile or even *yeeehawww* while skiing. Skiing is now in the top ten of my favorite activities, but it took a long time to attain this pleasure ranking.

Altitude can be an issue in the Cascades, at least on Mt. Rainier, an enormous volcano over 14,000 feet in elevation, with dozens of major routes. The problem stems from living one hundred feet or less above sea level in Seattle. Acclimation rate and degree seem hard-wired. Some people acclimate to altitude quicker and better than others. Acclimation doesn't necessarily depend on the degree of overall cardiovascular fitness.

I found out I needed time to acclimate to altitude on an attempt of Ptarmigan Ridge on Rainier, with Linda, Paul, and Ron. As we approached a high bivi at 10,000 feet, I felt sick and slowed to a plod. Paul asked what was wrong as he climbed past. Paul passing me was rare.

I described my symptoms, and he diagnosed, "You have acute mountain sickness; you need to go down." Descent is the most effective treatment.

We decided the others would continue while Linda, who felt fine, and I went down. We could rapidly glissade 3,000 feet to a lower bivi. I felt like crap the rest of the day. It depressed me the next morning to see our friends ascending this classic route. I resolved to never repeat my mountain sickness episode and take my time in climbing routes on Rainier. Later, living at higher altitudes in Canada and New Mexico, I experienced no problems at all on 14,000-foot peaks, although substantially higher peaks remained an issue.

Easy rock mountains can be dangerous. On an attempt of the classic Ptarmigan Traverse in the North Cascades, Linda, Paul, and I, along with another physician, climbed two easy peaks before we bailed due to bad weather. Being a multi-day trip, we didn't take helmets to reduce weight. This was silly. Helmets weigh little, but I think we also fell prey to the notion that technically easy rock peaks don't require such protection.

In reality, lower angled slopes on easy peaks often hold the greatest amount of loose rock. On Mt. Formidable, which isn't particularly formidable, after summitting we downclimbed a vertical chimney un-roped. Paul's friend released a tennis-ball size rock that collided with my bare noggin. It stunned me for a moment, but fortunately I hooked a finger through an old piton to keep from falling off.

The two docs reached me and commenced to argue about how to treat the gushing wound. I wiped my face off and voted to continue our descent and deal with the wound in camp. By then, the wound was clotted and I didn't worry about it. After this, I wore a helmet religiously, or I'd be dead by now. I've been hit on the head while wearing a helmet by countless rocks and ice chunks since.

And there was soloing easy climbs. When Linda and I were learning roped climbing with Paul and other friends, I didn't solo many technical routes in the Cascades. One notable exception was the West Ridge of Mt. Stuart, a tremendous granite peak in the eastern Cascades. Both Linda and Paul were out of town, so I went by myself. Although not technically difficult, it isn't a straightforward ridge route, and it's long.

Being early summer, the gullies on the West Ridge affording the easiest climbing were full of snow. I was inefficient: starting too late, carrying too much weight, trying to find the absolute easiest route, putting on and taking off crampons, and other time wasters. I decided to bail about three quarters of the way up. Rather than downclimbing the entire thing, which would've been much faster, I rapped many times, using up all of my nuts and *slings* (webbing loops) as anchors and almost stranding myself. Again, this was before cell phones.

My retreat was one of the few times in my climbing life I was close to self-imposed disaster, but I learned a set of valuable lessons. These included starting early, going light, just climbing instead of dicking around looking for the easiest path on a complex route, climbing snowy or icy rock with crampons, downclimbing rather than rapping, or simply finishing the damn thing and walking off the other side. I'd gone overboard on safe climbing practice and forgot I had complete confidence in soloing this level of difficult rock and snow. In compensation, Linda and I later returned and completed the superior classic North Ridge in good form and good time.

The only death I've witnessed in the mountains to date was while descending Chair Peak near Snoqualmie Pass with Paul and another physician. After summiting, we rapped a gully, and heard a large rockfall in an adjoining gully. Paul belayed me down so I could cross the intervening rib between gullies and investigate.

I reached the accident scene, and it was ugly. A party of two was ascending the gully, when a large rock flake weighing hundreds of pounds released and fell on the leader, crushing his helmeted head. His partner, who tried to help the injured climber, was covered in blood and completely freaked out.

I yelled to the two docs above for them to hurry the hell up. When they reached my position, they went into impressive wilderness doc action. I belayed them over to the party, and they examined the fallen climber.

Paul sadly observed, "If we were in the ER, we could intubate him, but we can't here." The victim died soon after. Paul's friend knew the victim, a fellow doc, but didn't recognize him due to his massive facial injuries.

Another guy who happened to be climbing the gully witnessed the accident and ran out to call the sheriff's office, but it was way too late. I doubt the surviving partner ever climbed again.

Death is a sad and sensitive subject, but for all of us it's just a matter of when, where, and how. An increase in the probability of early death from frequent climbing, especially difficult technical mountaineering, should be expected. Risk is cumulative. Yet, spouses, parents, and friends often seem shocked when a climber dies in the mountains. Maybe this is due to the difficulty most non-climbers have understanding the risks associated with climbing. I can describe them as best I can, but this doesn't substitute for direct experience. Linda would be sad, but wouldn't be shocked if I died or die in the mountains. Non-climbers also don't understand climbing's great rewards and addictive nature, and thus can't realistically judge the tradeoffs associated with the risk of death.

Some non-climbers, upon hearing of a climbing death, will say, "At least they died doing something they loved." That's like saying a person who enjoys driving a sports car wouldn't mind dying in a horrible car crash. Climbing deaths are often just as horrible. No sane climber wants to die climbing. I'd much rather die in bed loaded up on painkillers and surrounded by loved ones, or better yet in my sleep.

During this time, I worked in a lab at the University of Washington. The job had its risks. I worked with machines called flow cytometers, combining a dreadful mix of high-powered lasers, high voltage, and human bodily fluids. Plus sitting in front of a computer, which has probably damaged my body more than anything else over the years.

My professional career began with a graduate course in environmental risk assessment, free of charge because I worked for the university. Assessing and quantifying risks for a living sounded cool. The course focused on risks associated with toxicants in the environment. I quickly reckoned environmental risks to humans from low doses of most chemicals and radionuclides are often hypothetical or vastly overestimated, and thus create unnecessary fear among the public and the waste of hundreds of billions of dollars. The general concepts of risk assessment and analysis resonated with me, however. This course opened the door to a career in risk.

I earned a Master's degree in Environmental Health, and worked for a few years as a consultant. I then obtained most of a Ph.D. in Toxicology; "most" because Linda and I moved away from Seattle. There were other impediments such as my aversion to subservience, which is a typical state suffered by doctorate students. I'm considered *all but dissertation*, or a "Candidate in Philosophy," which sounds like somebody running for political office in ancient Greece. Despite partial certification, I built a successful academic and consulting career addressing a wide range of both hypothetical and real risks and risk management scenarios, until I retired in 2019.

One example of hypothetical versus actual risk was my evaluation of a Superfund site, a defunct cobalt and copper mine. At a meeting with US Environmental Protection Agency (EPA) staff, a bunch of lawyers, and the manager of the mine, EPA proposed a highly unlikely, hypothetical exposure scenario. It involved a teenager driving miles of rough roads up to the remote mine site, cutting the lock on the road's gate, climbing a high fence with barbed wire on top, trespassing on mine property, mucking around in contaminated dirt for a few hours, then returning home. Why a hypothetical teen might do such silly and illegal stuff wasn't made clear. Concerned about the teen's exposure to metals in the dirt, EPA wanted to use his estimated exposure level to come up with cleanup levels for the mine site, which in turn determined whether and how much the site would be remediated. In other words, they wanted to clean up the dirt so that hypothetical toxicity wouldn't transpire in the hypothetically trespassing teen.

When EPA presented this scenario to the group, the miner, a cig-smoking, flannel-shirt-in-a-room-of-suits, weather-beaten old coot, leaned back and sneered, "If I catch somebody trespassing on my mine property, they'll get a case of acute lead poisoning from my .30-06."

I busted out laughing, and he cackled in reply, but everybody else in the room got real serious-like and whispered among themselves.

I should've realized early on most environmental risk assessment involving hypothetical risk wasn't for me, but I somehow found myself making a living at it off and on for over twenty years. A consistent paycheck is a powerful motivator. I've no doubt my personal experiences contributed to my work-related views and approaches. Actual risk is more compelling to me than hypothetical risk. For example, as a consultant I evaluated catastrophic scenarios, preventing hundreds of potential deaths due to collapsing mines and exploding gas pipelines. I led an academic research program focused on assessing and reducing medical errors in a cancer treatment facility, saving patient lives.

Serious actual risks often arise in an unexpected fashion. While we lived there, Seattle experienced a dangerous incident involving food contamination, the 1993 hemorrhagic Escherichia coli bacterial outbreak. Over seven-hundred people, most in Washington, were infected with bacteria in beef patties contaminated with cow shit. Four children died and other victims suffered permanent injury including kidney and brain damage. Public health agencies traced the outbreak to a restaurant chain's "Monster Burger." A discount promotion used the perverse slogan "So good it's scary!" The burgers weren't cooked long enough or at a high enough temperature to kill the resident bacteria.

After this, Linda and I gave up eating beef. We didn't realize the devastating ecological and climate-change impacts of eating beef at the time, but those are other great reasons not to eat it. Chicken and pork soon fell by the wayside. We continued to eat fish and shellfish, because this was Seattle, after all. We cut out seafood when we moved and were vegetarians for twenty years, until backsliding in recent years for health reasons.

An uncontrollable, catastrophic risk associated with the Pacific Northwest is seismic. *The Really Big One* will strike at some point, and we considered this risk more carefully after experiencing a minor tremor in Seattle.

I hope The Really Big One doesn't occur in my lifetime. Aside from the death toll, this will significantly damage the US economy. It baffles me why so many Californians have moved to Seattle. I wonder why they aren't more seismically risk averse. I can't explain why fewer than fifteen percent of Californians and Washingtonians carry earthquake insurance on their homes, especially considering most of them live in high-risk areas, and the insurance doesn't cost much. Many people just seem to hope for the best. Intellectually, they realize disasters can happen, but don't seem to believe they or people they care about will be affected. This is an interesting cognitive phenomenon applicable to many risks.

Another Seattle-ish catastrophic risk is being smacked with foreign nukes. Puget Sound has a big red target on it, because it's relatively close to potential nukers to the west, it's a powerful economic engine, and there's a Trident nuclear-armed submarine base to the north. A major hit on Puget Sound would result in many direct deaths, infrastructure destruction, and economic damage. It would also spread a horrendous radioactive cloud to the east from both the blast as well as the highly radioactive material released from the Trident base, zapping a large swath of the US population.

Linda and I made some trips to nearby Canada while in Seattle. We backcountry skied in the Coast Range, such as the wonderful "Musical Bumps" from the Whistler ski area. One of the few places we've experienced true hip-deep powder snow was glacier skiing at Rogers Pass in the Columbia Mountains. We also made a half-hearted July climbing trip. The intent was to climb near Rogers Pass, but recent snowfall blanketed the area, a shock to our American climatic orientation. We drove further east and scrambled up the dog route on Mt. Temple near Lake Louise in a snowstorm and climbed some other easy peaks. The breathtaking scenery and the scale of the Canadian Rockies captured our imaginations.

My company's Calgary office offered me a transfer, and coincidentally the University of Calgary had a faculty position opening for Linda. I mentioned Seattle's seismic risk in an early discussion with a Canadian geologist who worked for the company, and his enthusiastic reply was, "That's the great thing about Calgary, eh? It's geologically stable!"

Linda and I decided to move north, eh, and the risks climbed much higher, through harder mountain doors.

Rapping into a crevasse on Mt. Baker, Washington, for some early ice climbing in the late 1980s. Must be a new helmet, as my target has only been hit a few times (credit: L. Cook).

Descent into the maelstrom. My mentor Paul skiing down into a whiteout on Mt. Rainier, Washington, as sunset approaches (credit: R. C. Lee).

Approaches in the Cascades, in this case to the Price Glacier on Mt. Shuksan in Washington, were sometimes the riskiest part of the climb. Crossing that slippery log taint easy with a big pack, and we really didn't want to fall in the raging river (credit: R. C. Lee).

Large avalanche caused by serac fall on the Coleman Headwall of Mt. Baker, Washington. This wiped out our footprints from ascending the wall several hours earlier (credit: R. C. Lee).

Their Cascadian eyes were bigger than their stomachs. Linda contemplating the Peuterey Ridge on Mont Blanc (left skyline), France. Large unstable cornices and avalanche risk caused us to bail on the Aiguille du Midi to Aiguille du Plan traverse (credit: R. C. Lee).

The Harder Mountain Door

LINDA AND I DRIVE BACK FROM AN ALPINE ROCK CLIMB ON CASTLE MOUNtain past the fantastical towers of Mt. Rundle, between Banff and Canmore. Camille Saint-Saëns' Symphony #3 is playing, and the first crushing pipe organ chord belts out, which never fails to tingle my spine. In a choked-up voice, I observe, "Behold the cathedrals of stone." Upon those rocks we build our church, and we approach the nave. We unlock the door to harder mountains.

We managed the most important risk of moving to another country by lining up jobs and work permits in advance. We probably wouldn't have been able to immigrate to Canada at all if we hadn't done this, but moving to another country without a job or substantial financial reserves could be rather dicey if things didn't work out. Canada was also expensive relative to the US, with high taxes. This was offset by nice benefits, such as inexpensive health care. Buying lots of cozy clothes managed the risk of freezing our buns off.

Cultural and social differences were an unexpected risk. Many Americans consider Canada a sort of colder and darker United States. We were partial prey to this myth. In reality, it's a quite different country in history, demographics, language, and so on. There's often an underlying competitive attitude toward Americans and, in some cases, frank anti-American bias. We adapted, though. For example, I learned to speak faster so people wouldn't finish my Southern, slack-jaw-drawled sentences for me, and I became more polite. We picked up some Canadian-isms, British-isms, and French-isms. We learned pronunciations such as *sore-y* for *sah-ry,* and *process* for *prah-cess.* Indeed, we became Canadian citizens.

Climbing in Canada required some adjustment. For example, we learned to be careful with technical difficulty and length ratings for Canadian Rockies climbs, due to Canadian understatement. Many American climbers have been spanked hard in the Canadian Rockies.

During an interview trip to Calgary, we wanted to climb a short easy peak. We bought a Rockies guidebook featuring "selected alpine climbs." In some cases, however, the guidebook's details were wrong, calling into question whether the author had even been near a particular mountain. In most cases, the guidebook understated the difficulties in our Cascades, if not Alps experience. And it wasn't just us. Canadian climbers often referred to this guidebook as *Selected Sandbags* or *The Book of Lies*.

The route we chose on Mt. Edith near Banff was described in *Sandbags* as "very popular with beginners." This was encouraging but untrue. We found the route with difficulty. Due to its unpopularity, a clear trail didn't exist, and I launched off leading with my typical Cascades alpine rack of a few cams, nuts, and slings. The climbing was indeed easy, but the problem was my pro fit few of the cracks. Typical cracks were a small fraction of an inch in width. I carried no *knifeblade* or thin pitons and no hammer, and indeed had never hammered in any sort of piton, but this is the appropriate pro for such thin cracks. The limestone was prickly and solid, and I ended up soloing the pitches and bringing Linda up at belays. It was disconcerting, but manageable.

Then we descended. The description of the scrambling descent route sounded convoluted, and we noted a rap station, so we launched off the other side of the peak with our doubled one-hundred-sixty-foot rope. This was a mistake. The first couple of raps went fine, but then we reached a ledge above a large wall. I couldn't determine the vertical distance, but it looked much longer than eighty feet. Few things would've been worse than to rap down a blind cliff face and find myself with no ledge or anchor. I would then have had to climb back up a face that may or may not have been climbable, or climb the rope using *prussiks* or cords tied around the rope, which isn't easy.

And it was getting dark. We'd underestimated the amount of time the approach and climb would take, being so "popular with beginners," and all. Clever Linda suggested I traverse along the ledge and determine if an alternative way down existed. I found an old piton in a loose chimney, backed the piton up with a nut, rigged a rap, and we escaped. We arrived at the car in darkness.

Upon returning to Seattle and relating the episode to a dude who'd climbed in Canada, he exclaimed, "What, you didn't have your Canadian Rockies escape kit?" He suggested this should include an ice hammer, a fistful of pitons, many yards of *tat* (thin nylon webbing), two two-hundred-foot ropes, and in some cases ice screws.

We learned our lesson. We also didn't account for the wildlife, including grizzlies, wolves, and cougars. Yet another reason the Cascades are soft mountains in comparison. They don't have nearly the biota that can eat you.

Using a canine analogy, the Rockies are snarling Pitbulls compared to the gentle Golden Retrievers of the Cascades. They can involve just about every possible source of mountain risk I can think of, aside from high altitude and hordes of people: remote locations, large elevation gains, loose rock, icy rock, lack of rock pro, glaciers with yawning crevasses, crappy snow, cold temperatures, changeable weather, large wildlife, and on and on.

A world-class climber later told me, "If you can handle the Canadian Rockies safely, you can climb anywhere in the world."

Thus, began almost ten years of working and climbing in Canada, starting in 1998. We did little else. Linda and I both worked decent-paying, full-time jobs with good benefits. So, our time in Calgary was at last financially stable, a nasty risk monkey off our backs. It only took us four decades to get there, but we never received substantial financial help from anybody. Late Boomers, indeed, but we earned every dollar and loonie ourselves.

A big advantage of climbing in the Canadian Rockies is we didn't have to backpack to many areas. We could climb hundreds of small- to large-scale routes in a day from the Trans-Canada Highway, the Icefields Parkway, Lake Louise, and similar access points. Admittedly, those "days" often went into double-digit-hours. Starting out in the dark and returning in the dark wasn't uncommon, although we tried to avoid the latter. We could also helicopter into more remote areas, albeit at a cost.

As in the Mt. Edith experience, part of the steep learning curve in the Canadian Rockies involved dealing with types of rock different than we'd experienced in the Cascades or elsewhere. Most of the main spine of the Rockies originated as ancient seabed and consists of limestone, dolomite, or quartzite. We were amazed when we found ourselves climbing on fossils. Any type of rock could range from solid to appallingly *chossy* (loose).

Few climbs had good permanent pro such as expansion bolts. There were often clusters of *manky* (loose or unreliable) pitons for belays and raps. I became manky-averse after I popped an old piton out on a rappel off Mt. Lougheed. I'd backed the piton up with another piton or I wouldn't be writing this memoir. I didn't even trust older rap bolts and backed them up. I always felt a great sense of relief and refuge, however, when I saw a bolted station at the top of a tough pitch, or a few yards before the bottom end of the ropes on a rap.

The limestone route named Joy on the peak with the wonderful name, Mt. Indefatigable, taught me a valuable lesson. Climbing steep friction slabs often made me uncomfortable, and most of this 2000-foot climb is steep and slabby. Friction climbing is like climbing a steep pitched roof, relying solely on your soles' friction rather than nice hand and footholds.

The first time we attempted the route, the *runouts* (long stretches with no pro) were disconcerting. Losing it meant a long sliding fall on cheese-grater limestone. Robert-burger would've been the result, an unpleasant death indeed. I backed off early even though the climbing itself wasn't difficult. It differed from anything we'd tried before, although Linda never had much issue with slabs. I hate backing off due to my own lack of competency, so we returned. The experience of just sucking it up and friction-climbing the tremendous runout slabs on Joy was akin to my mushroom experience when I crossed the shaky log. It liberated me. If I simply maintained good balance and form, I wouldn't be ground into Robert-burger.

I was joyous I'd climbed through the door of slab climbing, particularly because many rock and mountaineering routes in the Rockies involve such climbing.

Even confidence on slabs has limits, as I found out soloing Mt. Fable for the first time in early season. Yep, I soloed. Sometimes Linda was busy, or I just wanted to get out alone. My chosen route involved easy slab climbing, but in this case the easiest lines, runnels or water-worn grooves in the limestone, were full of ice and snow. I wore smooth-soled rock shoes, so this forced me to take harder lines than I liked. Like many routes in the Rockies, it would've been riskier trying to descend what I'd just climbed than to just continue and scramble down the easiest side. This is a situation known as *the only way down is up*. Another lesson learned: don't try to push the season too much in the Rockies if only prepared for rock climbing.

Worse, were face-first scrambling descents with no pro, down ball bearing-sized gravel covered sloping slabs with cliffs below, while wearing stiff mountain boots as well as crampons, if snowed or iced up. Think about gingerly walking down a steep, slick, gravely, skyscraper roof with metal points on your boots and no safety harness. It was tense at times.

Chossy rock was perhaps the greatest challenge on many of the rock peaks. The long Perren Route on Mt. Whyte was "an easy day out," according to *Sandbags*, yet another lie. It took us twelve hours car-to-car. I pulled off a microwave-sized rock on this route and threw it to the side to avoid hitting Linda, all while avoiding falling off in the process.

The Northwest Ridge of Mt. Blane is cool-looking, but appearances can be deceiving. Halfway up my non-Linda partner became alarmed, as the descent is down the same ridge. Most handholds on this route were moveable, and using a rope caused rockfall. According to *Sandbags*, Mt. Blane "has an undeserved reputation for 'horrible' and 'horrendous' rock." Nope, it's deserved. It's a steep technical knife-edge constructed of loose bricks. Strangely, I learned to accept this sort of thing and flow with it. I encouraged my partner that we needed to get to the top first, then we'd worry about getting back down the ridge. By the time we summited and were off the ridge, he was knackered from fatigue and stress, but I jacked him up with an energy drink and energy gel and we hiked out.

I complained about the *Book of Lies* route descriptions to a mountain guide after several such trips. He laughed and suggested I should just copy or cut out the photos and carry them, ignoring the sandbag-gy text. Linda and I subsequently followed this advice.

On Pilot Mountain in early season, I pulled up on a frozen, yard-wide chockstone wedged in a chimney. It had been in place for many years. Much to my surprise the chockstone released, striking my thigh just above my knee; I shoved it to the side to avoid killing Linda. We completed the scramble, now easier due to my removal of the several-hundred-pound chockstone. I have a scar to remind me of the bastard.

Choss was also an issue on descents. Pulling a rope down after rapping could release volleys of everything from pebbles to boulders. Chopping the rope from rockfall was a concern, not to mention being killed. I owned several rock-shortened ropes after a couple of years of Canadian Rockies climbing.

I could go on, but most of the mishaps we experienced on rock peaks were inconsequential. An exception was on Chinaman's Peak looming over Canmore, now more appropriately named after the Chinese gentleman Ha Ling. Back in the day, he first walked up the dog route.

Linda and I launched off early on the 1,500-foot Northeast Face. Perhaps halfway up, as I pondered the easiest route, I spied an old piton and a bolt. I clipped the rope to them. As I headed up from this pro, a pair of young Canmore *ass-guides* (aspirant or assistant mountain guides, in mountain guide parlance) caught up to us. They suggested I should traverse right from the anchors, and I made the mistake of assuming they knew what they were talking about.

I climbed right, determined the ass-guides were full of shit, and traversed back. I made a second mistake of stepping on a rock nubbin without testing it. It released, and I fell ten feet on the good double anchor, stripping my hands on the cheese-grater limestone in the process.

Linda lowered me back down to the belay ledge, and the ass-guides had the gall to ask if I wanted a rescue.

I politely replied, "No thanks, you go ahead," but thought, *Get the hell out of my presence before I throw your asses off.*

I taped up my bleeding hands with hockey tape, put on a pair of gloves, took some acetaminophen with codeine, and we rapped down. I couldn't climb with such peeled and painful hands. I went back later with another partner and completed the route, as it no longer interested Linda.

Aside from my un-roped fall in North Carolina, this was my only consequential *whipper* on rock. If I'd been soloing, which plenty of expert climbers do on this route, I would've died. The only long-term consequence of this fall involves scars on my left wrist that look like I tried to off myself. I sometimes get funny looks when people notice these.

A musician friend subsequently observed I should take better care of my valuable hands covered with *gobies* (wounds), so I started to slack off on pure rock climbing a little after this. My hands are possibly my most valued body parts.

Linda wasn't immune to accidents. After a long and arduous approach over multiple glaciers and thousands of feet of scrambling, we ascended most of remote Mt. Selwyn to find an impassable *'schrund* (a large crevasse or *bergschrund*) in the glacier near the top.

We gave up and scrambled back down steep loose terrain. At the steepest rock section, I set up a rap on a block of stone five feet square by tying a long piece of nylon tat around it. I examined the rock, kicked it a few times, and it seemed solid. I rapped down with no problem, hung out on a ledge, and waited for Linda to arrive. Arrive she did, but in a much more rapid fashion than I.

She flew past, with a barrage of rock following her, and landed on her back on a ledge forty or fifty feet below. I grabbed the rope as she flew past, surprisingly without shredding my hands, but this was one reason she stopped.

I called out to her, but got no response, as the fall had knocked the wind out of her. After running down scrambling terrain to reach her, we determined she was unhurt. She had landed on her pack and wore a helmet. The entire anchor block sheared off, as the tat was still tied in an intact loop.

If she'd fallen off either side of the ridge, she would've died. After this event, we began to take the possibility of rescue more seriously. If Linda had been alive but immobile, there was no way I could've carried her out over miles of glacier and scrambling terrain. It would've taken me at least a full day to get out alone, if I didn't fall in a crevasse. And since cell phone coverage didn't exist in this area, we didn't even carry phones.

As soon as we got back, I bought a satellite phone. Expensive, but being able to call a helicopter is an important risk management strategy.

A common bit of conventional wilderness wisdom is to inform a responsible person of your plans: where you are going and when you plan to return. It seems like a good idea, but we found it to be impractical in the Canadian

Rockies, or most other areas for that matter. Even after cell phones became ubiquitous, substantial coverage holes existed in many mountain areas. We would've been constantly trying to call somebody rather than climbing, as we often just drove around in the summer looking for *sucker holes* (transient spots with good weather), grabbing peaks wherever we could. And the Canadian Rockies National Parks have good rescue teams.

In most of the American West for example, climbers are frankly on their own anyway, and quick rescue is illusory. We gave up telling people where we planned on climbing and relied on our own abilities and being able to call out using a sat phone. We persist in this to the present day.

We carry rescue insurance, providing access to professional rescue capability. We also have the phone numbers of emergency physicians who teach and practice wilderness medicine. Sat phones and similar devices can fail, however. Aside from the device itself or battery failing, it's often difficult to find a signal in narrow canyons. In order to get a signal, a satellite must be orbiting directly above the narrow slot of sky. In such country, we're mindful of the Danny Boyle movie *127 Hours*.

A far more important strategy is choosing a good climbing partner or partners. A good partner is the absolute best piece of safety hardware a climber can have. Paul, Ron, my Canadian friend Adam, and a few others were good partners, but I was extremely lucky to have such a partner in Linda, with the bonus that she's my love and mate for life. She's experienced dozens of situations with equanimity that have literally scared the shit out of other climbers.

As an example, on Brewer's Buttress on Castle Mountain north of Banff, a couple of guys were ahead of us gearing up for the first pitch. They'd spent the night in a small hut on a ledge near the beginning of the route, and Linda and I started from the car.

The other team's primary position didn't last long, as the dude leading the first pitch screamed and fell off, out of our sight. Although he wasn't injured, they rapped off the route. As soon as the leader hit the ground, he immediately ran off for urgent excretory business. It wasn't clear why he fell, but aside from soiling the mountain environment he appeared to be okay. They indicated they were no longer keen on this route and headed down.

We launched off, all by ourselves, on one of the finest moderate alpine rock routes in the Rockies and a great day in the mountains.

The big glaciated Canadian mountains posed big challenges. I could've sworn these monsters were actively trying to kill us at times, but Linda and I climbed through their giant doors regardless.

We wanted to climb the classic snow and ice Skyladder route on Mt. Andromeda. We reached the 'schrund at the base of the route. As I poked my helmeted head up over the edge, a shotgun blast of pebbles whizzed by at terminal velocity, slower than shot but fast enough to cause damage if they connected. So, we backed up and climbed up the North Bowl instead, a superb sweep of snow and ice with no rock in sight.

We flowed up the face, simul-climbing with ice screws inserted into the glacier ice between us at all times to stop a potential fall. Seracs were an issue, however. As we neared the top of the face, a serac the size of a bungalow released fifty yards to our right, crashing to the glacier below. Due to our monkeying around trying to find a route that wouldn't kill us, we reached the ridge leading to the summit later than I liked.

When I suggested we should immediately descend, Linda replied, "Get your sorry ass to the summit." With this encouragement we continued and summited. The icy wilderness of the Columbia Icefields and surrounding peaks was magnificent.

We thought we'd escaped the whizzing rocks. The rap descent was down a steep icy glacier between Mts. Andromeda and Athabasca. I clipped into an ice screw above the 'schrund, and shortly after, a rock the size of a lacrosse ball hit my Spectra and carbon fiber helmet, stunning me for a moment and cracking the helmet. The rock fell in front of my boot, and I picked it up. I kept the bastard as a reminder.

Mt. Robson is the tallest peak in the Canadian Rockies, and a beautiful but dangerous mountain rarely climbed due to continual bad weather. Like many big mountains, it creates its own weather patterns. A lenticular cloud cap can form on the mountain resulting in whiteout and windy conditions. It's easy to step off a cliff or cornice or get blown off into oblivion in such conditions. According to Mt. Robson Provincial Park about ten percent of Robson attempts are successful, although this statistic is based on reported climbs and therefore the true percentage may be less. Climbers are likely biased toward reporting climbs they complete, as opposed to ones they bail from.

Linda and I chose the relatively straightforward and classic Kain Route. This is named after the pioneering Conrad Kain. Kain guided the first ascent, rather incredibly, in 1913, wearing tweeds and hobnailed boots and chopping steps for his guests the entire way using a long ice ax.

The climb involves a long hiking approach, extensive glacier travel to a base camp, climbing a 1,600-foot, over fifty-degree snow and ice slope called the Kain Face, and another thousand vertical feet of corniced steep snow and ice ridge to the summit. The descent usually reverses this route. Most parties allow a week to climb the mountain to allow for the approach, the climb and descent, and delays due to bad weather.

We decided to avoid the hiking approach by flying via helicopter to a bivi site near the Kain Face. This maximized our chance of success given a limited weather window, but it introduced a new set of risks associated with flying in a mountain environment. The expense and the risk of flying were outweighed by the avoidance of a twenty-mile hike with sixty-pound backpacks and travel across a heavily crevassed glacier, which was impassible anyway at the time due to recent major serac fall.

Some climbers engage in ethical handwringing regarding an aerial means of approach, suggesting climbers should eschew any means of approach aside from hiking, but this is silly. Such ethical purists have obviously never been to the Alps, where climbers can take ski lifts to access hundreds of world-class routes. Or perhaps they haven't flown into remote areas of the Canadian Rockies, British Columbia Coast Range, Alaska, and many other places where climbers have to schlep big loads for a week or much more to even get close to a destination peak. On the other hand, not many climbers are as pure as the late great Goran Kropp, who bicycled from Sweden to Mt. Everest, climbed it solo and unsupported by porters, and cycled back.

A major source of uncertainty was the weather. Based on climate statistics, a better-than-even probability of nasty weather existed. After waiting a couple of days climbing elsewhere in the general area, a three-day, good-weather window opened, and we flew through it. We set up a bomber tent and reinforced it by building snow walls around it. A tent getting blown off the mountain wasn't a trivial risk. For the climb itself, we decided to take the clothes on our backs, two two-hundred-foot ropes, a minimum of pro and other stuff, and enough food and water considering replenishment with snow to sustain us for approximately twenty hours. We remembered Chouinard and didn't carry bivi gear, as we could climb faster when lighter, and a bivi on this route wouldn't be pleasant at all if it started weatherin'.

We awoke to a clear, starry sky, a critical decision-point, at two a.m. and trotted to the Kain Face. No choice but to give'r. There are many, much-bigger snow and ice faces in the world, but the face looked pretty damn steep and big when we faced it. By comparison, The Wall in the *Game of Thrones* fantasy saga was less than half the height.

We were the first on the route that season, which meant no nice steps to follow in the lower angled snow. For efficiency and speed, we chose a steep line on the right-hand side of the Face; the most direct and iciest route to the summit ridge. The snow would've been more arduous and slower. However, this icy line was exposed to substantial serac fall risk. We managed this by completing the Face before the sun rose. It would've been much riskier to climb this line later in the day. We flowed up the Face, simul-climbing with ice screws as running pro. It's spooky climbing such a route with head-lamps, especially the lame lamps of the day, as we couldn't see far until the moonless sky brightened. The later invention of kick-ass LED headlamps was an innovation making such climbing safer.

As we climbed, a cloud cap started to form, intensifying the need for speed. By this time, the snow on the ridge was knee-deep and climbing fast was difficult. The ridge near the top consisted of gargoyle-like formations of insubstantial and unprotectable ice. I was tired and a little apprehensive, but Linda once again said, "Get your sorry ass to the summit." She didn't want to have to return. With this encouragement, we summited. Good thing she was there. We couldn't spend much time enjoying the amazing panorama, as we immediately started our descent due to the sinking of the cloud cap and worsening weather.

We rapped a couple of times off the steeper top part of the Face, but then just started downclimbing with two tools to hurry things up. We made it back to camp fifteen hours after starting, with the mountain now immersed in cloud. We'd been alone on the mountain the entire time.

When we arrived at our tent, a couple of wiped-out Brits who showed up gave us a hard time about our icy ascent line up the Face, saying it was "dangerous," a real buzzkill. It was a silly argument; all mountains and routes are dangerous. They'd been scared off the North Face, which looked in perfect condition to me when we flew in, and then they traversed through a nightmare of seracs and crevasses to our bivi site, so their opinion was worthless. I was too tired to even reply with a, "Piss off, hosers."

In contrast, a mountain guide who had helicoptered in with his party offered us tea and commented, "You summited, and you're alive, so congratulations." Cheers, brother!

The weather deteriorated and we needed to recover, so we spent the next day at our base camp. The guided party spent twenty hours on the mountain and still didn't summit. We had previously decided not to fly out due to the expense. The weather wasn't conducive for flying anyway. We also wanted to experience one of the most scenic hikes in the Canadian Rockies on the way out. Unfortunately, we needed to bypass the typical route down the upper Robson Glacier due to dangerous teetering seracs the size of houses, and take a more circuitous and unpleasant descent ridge involving exposed loose rock climbing with heavy packs.

When we attained the lower glacier, I tried to walk a direct line across while probing for hidden crevasses with a ski pole, but I wasn't wearing the pole strap. I poked through a snow bridge over a large hidden crevasse and the pole disappeared without a trace down the seemingly bottomless hole. I used Linda's for the remainder of the glacier, but I wore the damn strap. A day's worth of heavily crevassed glacier travel and a long day's trail hike later, we arrived at the car.

The mental relief associated with being off such a mountain and in a hot tub is indescribable.

After this experience, Linda and I developed a paper on rational risk management approaches in mountaineering, based on some work with Canadian professionals and our own experiences. We used our climb of Mt. Robson as a case study. We published it as a book chapter, and I presented this work at the Society for Risk Analysis annual conference. The talk received more interest and positive feedback than any other presentation I'd made at the conference over twenty-plus years.

A former head of the Harvard Center for Risk Analysis came up to me afterward and marveled, "You really live this risk management stuff, don't you?"

I replied, "Yep, I'd probably be dead by now if I didn't."

Whiteouts were also common on the Columbia Icefields, which host many large peaks. Linda and I skied there several times, planning to climb peaks; in all cases, whiteouts occurred, and we just sat in the tent for two or three days before getting bored and skiing out. I never would've been successful as a true expedition climber; I didn't have the patience.

The easiest access to the main Icefields is up the Athabasca Glacier. To gain the Icefields, there's the choice of either skiing up the glacier itself through a major crevasse field or hugging the right side under the gigantic and often falling death-seracs of Mt. Snowdome. Due to the risk of whiteouts, we stuck yard-long bamboo wands tied with surveyor's flagging in the snow along the ascent route so we could follow it back. Unfortunately, we could only carry so many wands, and sometimes they blew over or became buried.

We skied up one spring with a couple of friends with the intent of climbing several peaks. We observed recent serac fall off Mt. Snowdome, and not wanting to be crushed by tons of falling ice, we placed wands at one- or two-hundred feet intervals wandering up the middle of the glacier. We thought it sufficient for route finding.

Once we gained the main plateau, we observed a line of wolverine tracks heading off over miles of crevassed terrain toward the Saskatchewan Glacier. I hope it made it. We then sat the obligatory three days in the tents in a whiteout storm, waking up every hour or so to shovel snow to prevent the tents from being crushed.

We descended the same route without climbing a damn thing. Skiing uphill while roped wasn't a big deal, as we walked with *climbing skins* on the bottom of the skis to provide traction. Skiing downhill while roped was a different matter; it could be frustrating at the least and an amusing but dangerous shit-show at the worst. We un-roped but couldn't see all the wands. We were forced to peer intently into the clouds and try to divine the location of the next wand, and not fall into a hidden crevasse.

Ron, skiing behind me, broke through a crevasse snow bridge and fell in. Falling in a crevasse is often fatal if the victim is unroped. However, Ron was able to bridge the edges of the slot with his arms and wedged his skis to the walls. The hole was thirty or more feet deep, and he didn't look happy at all.

I retrieved a rope, clipped him off, and the others anchored the rope while I tried to remember how to set up a pulley system to extract him. Ron was about my size and wore a big pack and skis, so he probably weighed two-hundred-fifty pounds. Pulleys, a wonderful invention, allow a rescuer to lift much more weight on a rope than otherwise. Due to Ron's obvious state of alarm and my impatience with the kerfuffle, I found it easier to just reach down, grab his arms, and haul him out while I was anchored and the others kept the rope tight. We roped up and navigated the remainder from memory and the wands we could see.

On subsequent trips, on crevassed glaciers not covered by a safe snow depth, Linda and I carried more wands and skied down while roped.

Another weather-related risk is lightning. We weathered many Canadian Rockies and Columbia Mountains summer thunderstorms while huddled in tents, which typically have metal poles. We'd often sleep cozied up with a bunch of metal climbing equipment we didn't want to leave outside the tent. Marmots have a chewing jones for the nylon bits. It was often hard to sleep at all in such storms.

On an approach to the North Face of Mt. Athabasca, the clouds rolled in, the ice tools on our packs started buzzing, and Linda's hair rose, a sign of an imminent lightning strike. We hauled ass as fast as we could (after snapping a photo of her hair of course) down the glacial *moraine* (rocks and gravel at the edge of a glacier) with stiff plastic boots and thirty-pound packs. We arrived at the car just in time to avoid being zapped and soaked.

Worse, a storm during a technical traverse of Mt. Hermit in the Columbia Mountains west of the major Rockies spine. We chose this peak because a nearby first choice, Mt. Tupper, had a party ahead of us. The clouds rolled in, and we saw a large lightning bolt strike Tupper's summit. Presumably the other party hadn't summited yet, or they would've been toast.

We thought we'd dodged the electric bullet, but no, the storm headed our way. We were descending from the summit on a sharp, exposed ridge when the trekking poles and ice axes stashed on our packs started to buzz, and we had to make a critical decision. Mt. Hermit, like most of the peaks in the area, is quartzite, a relatively smooth rock which can be slimy when wet. The quartzite in the area is also covered with even slimier "motor-oil" lichen, a descriptor used in the local guidebook. It started to rain. Did we hunker down and wait for the lightning and rain to stop, which could've been for days, or get the hell off in a hurry? Even stopping to rig raps would've wasted time. I don't think we've ever downclimbed technical terrain so quickly.

Crowding was usually not an issue in Canada, but there were exceptions. The first time Linda and I attempted the superlative quartzite Northwest Ridge of Mt. Sir Donald, we made the mistake of being there on a nice sunny summer weekend when it was packed with people. The crowding was likely due to this route's inclusion in a famous old book, Steve Roper and Alan Steck's *50 Classic Climbs of North America*. The featured climbs are often referred to as the "50 Crowded Classics." Sir Donald may indeed be one of the most crowded big technical peaks in Canada. It's relatively easy climbing, and has solid rock and a good approach trail.

We bivied below the peak before the ascent day and, coincidentally, ran into an older guy from Seattle planning to solo climb. He sounded and looked competent, and we even had some mutual friends, so we agreed he could join us.

He was a skilled climber, but this route freaked him out. The climbing difficulty isn't hard and the rock is superb, but this route is a lengthy knife-sharp ridge with tremendous exposure on either side. Climbers need to stay on the tippy-top to avoid rock deterioration on either side off the ridge. This guy was just overly careful and glacially slow.

In order to get up and down before dark, climbers need to: short-rope, in which the leader keeps the second on a short length of rope so they can be jerked into place if they slip, simul-climb roped with pro in between the climbers, or solo. The guidebook for this area, which doesn't sandbag or lie, states if a team is belaying the first few pitches, they need to back off.

The technique is too slow and they'll be benighted. Again, our companion was freaked out. He was a member of the regressive Seattle climbing tribe, unaccustomed to radical Alpen techniques such as simul-climbing, which have existed for as long as people have been using ropes in the mountains.

I estimated at least thirty people were on the route, going up or coming down. It was uncomfortably reminiscent of the Alps, and a shock, given we rarely encountered anybody else on Canadian peaks. People were acting like this was their first mountain, such as descending with ripped pants because they were scooting along on their butts instead of using their hands and feet. Climber-released rocks were flying all over the place. It was one of the riskiest situations we'd yet encountered in the mountains.

Our partner's discomfort, combined with the number of people clogging up the route and slowing us down, caused us to retreat. Linda and I returned later and climbed the route mid-week from the campground, which involved a soul-crushing 7,800-foot elevation gain, but we were lazy and didn't want to carry overnight gear again. There were only two other widely spaced parties on the route. It was amazingly good climbing, and one of our favorite peaks.

❧

There are lots of large animals in the Canadian Rockies. Linda and I never experienced any close grizzly bear encounters, probably because there aren't many bears, and the Canadian National Parks do a good job of closing off areas to people when bears are active. We came close, though. Upon summiting Mt. Aberdeen and the adjoining Mt. Haddo near Lake Louise, we faced a choice of an arduous descent back down the snow and ice face or scrambling off the other side into the aptly named Paradise Valley.

The problem was, the valley was closed due to bear activity. We didn't see any Park Wardens and it was getting late, so we opted for the valley. Sure enough, as soon as we gained the valley trail a big steamy pile of fresh grizzly poo presented itself. We retrieved our ice tools and conceived a plan if we encountered a bear: We'd link arms and brandish our tools like a wickedly clawed, two-headed monster. We haven't tested this strategy to date.

On an approach in the same area in early season with a foot of snow on the ground, we retreated from the peak due to avalanche risk and discovered a cougar had stalked us for over a mile. There were no tracks when we first hiked in. We had no clue. We also saw a number of feline tails waving above long meadow grass on a summer approach to the rock peak Mt. Ishbel. We didn't want to encounter the mother and her kittens again. After we climbed the peak, we decided to descend and hike out a different and much longer route in order to avoid them. It also prompted me to start carrying a large knife if we weren't carrying ice tools. People have been killed by cougars in the Rockies. A Robert-sized kittycat was not a trivial risk.

Some Americans have asked why I didn't carry a firearm in these areas. Firearms are heavy, and Canadian authorities don't take kindly to anybody packing in their National Parks. That was even the case in the Yukon, where Linda and I backpacked for a week in Kluane National Park. This trek was almost entirely on grizzly and moose trails, often in heavy bush and forest. I've never wanted a rifle so bad in my life, but we satisfied ourselves with ice axes, magnum-sized cans of bear spray, and the hope the wind didn't blow. We were fortunate we didn't close-encounter any large animals. To alert them, we sang every song we knew until we were hoarse. I also frequently practiced with *bear bangers*, loud noisemakers similar to firecrackers intended to scare off a charging bear. I just needed to ensure the banger landed in front of the bear rather than behind it, thus practice was wise.

I was accustomed to large bears in Alaska and Canada, but wolves were a novel experience in the Canadian Rockies. We'd often see their tracks in the snow, and they were big. Wolves are shy though, and usually not seen. An exception was during an ostensible ice climbing trip in midwinter to the Ghost River area, a remote wilderness containing a huge number of rock and waterfall ice climbs. We drove in most of the way but were in danger of high-centering on large snow drifts. We left the packs and ice tools in the vehicle and, armed with ski poles, hiked to an area we hadn't explored. Unfortunately, I'd left my camera in the vehicle as well.

The trail we hiked was a summer, off-highway vehicle track through thin forest. After a couple of miles, I saw movement in the woods, and remarked to Linda, "Look at that giant coyote." She replied, "I don't think that's a coyote."

The wolf wasn't alone; we counted at least ten individuals, and there were likely more. We entered a sort of wolfish playground clearing, evidenced by the large number of tracks in the snow, but the furiously yipping and howling wolves stayed in the woods. I reminded myself wolf attacks are rare, but there we were, a couple of miles from our vehicle, in a remote area thirty miles from the nearest ranch, in midwinter, unarmed, alone with a Canadian wolfpack.

Drawing on our experience with dogs, which was the best we could think of at the time, we both picked up rocks, brandished our ski poles, and picked up our pace a bit, but didn't run. We didn't want to convey the appearance of prey. It worked out fine, although the effectiveness of throwing rocks at and pole-whipping an attacking wolfpack remains unclear. When time came to return, I thought we could skirt around the wolfish playground. This was difficult due to heavy bush, so we were forced to walk by them again. Everything was cool though, and this was one of the most magical experiences we've had with wildlife.

The wolves allowed us to peek through their secret door.

ॐ

"The journey is the thing" doesn't apply to modern air travel. I loathe flying in commercial jets, especially to international destinations. My aversion to flying is attributable to travel discomfort, not risk. I couldn't fly first-class while employed, unless somebody else was paying for it. Airline security drives me nuts; it's inefficient and ineffective. Flying also results in a shocking amount of carbon emissions. Regardless, Linda and I occasionally sucked it up and flew for the international rewards.

My first exposure to Scotland, aside from the fact of my partial heritage, was in winter. As part of my Canadian job, I worked with the National Health Service and a university in Newcastle-upon-Tyne, England. I'd managed to wrangle a first-class ticket out of them, which was golden with regard to reducing aerial discomfort. Newcastle is a terminus of Hadrian's Wall and might as well be Scotland; it had absolutely foul weather with snow, rain, *snain,* and everything *in betwain.* It was cold in Fort William, Scotland further north, which meant I wanted to go ice climbing. This was the main birthplace of modern ice and mixed climbing in the 1970s.

The first challenge was getting there. It's a five-hour drive from Newcastle in summer. I tried to find a 4WD vehicle, but the only option was an expensive Land Rover, so I opted for a front-wheel drive sedan and a shovel, and hoped the gravel-spreading *gritters* were busy.

The roads weren't bad, although driving was tense compared to my North American, wide-road experience. I became accustomed to wrong-side driving, but the tolerances were unreal. Sometimes, less than a foot existed between a rock wall and a careening-lorry hard place. Going as fast as possible at all times seemed to be the law. Roundabouts were exercises in shooting-the-gaps and hoping for the best.

Driving in the United Kingdom was probably the riskiest part of the trip, especially when the combined effects of speed and alcohol on the part of other drivers were considered. The National Health Service had recently drafted the astounding recommendation that British subjects should consume twenty-one drinks per week or less. It's a wonder more Brits don't die of liver failure.

Additional factors increased the risk of this expedition: I'd been away from Linda for two weeks and I was gloomy. The foul weather and winter darkness didn't help my funk, but the Jay Roach movie *Meet the Fockers* was playing at a tiny local theater, so this was a slight respite from the gloom. I developed excruciating tooth pain and needed a root canal. Everybody I revealed this to exclaimed, "*Don't* go to a Scottish dentist." I went to one for a pain medication prescription, and he wrote one for oxycodone. I suffered with a horrible cold, and thus took medication for this ailment. I was less than fit, as I'd been working in Newcastle with little real exercise.

I wasn't in the best condition for climbing, much less so for the partaking of wee drams due to the drugs. Combining Scotch and acetaminophen is a great recipe for liver damage. An additional discomfort was the lack of a shower in the bed-and-breakfast, and by god I'm a shower man. However, winter conditions in the hills were the best in ten years, so dammit, I went climbing.

Ben Nevis is the highest peak in Scotland. It's only a little over 4,000 feet, but it's a challenging mountain in winter. It looks like a giant whale, with a long and rounded body comprising the dog route, and a steep 2,300-foot high chopped off mouth, the glacier-carved Northeast Face. This complex rock face is exposed to the full force of North Atlantic gales, and if the temperature is cold, the routes can accumulate snow, *verglas* (ice on rock), and *rime* (frozen atmospheric moisture). There's also waterfall ice in some gullies. I set off to climb something on this classic face.

Fort William is about the same latitude as Fort McMurray, Alberta, which is way the hell up there, and I was there in winter. This meant approaching in the dark. I got up at five a.m., ate some miserable gruel, and took my oxy and some cold medication. I drove to Glen Nevis, a lovely pastoral valley where parts of the *Harry Potter* movies were filmed.

I started trudging up the trail, subject to shotgun blasts of *graupel* (rime pellets) driven by a powerful wind. A portent of things to come: Numerous sheep lay hunkered down, their eyes glowing in my headlamp beam. These were Scottish Highland sheep, for godssake. I should've taken a hint from their hunkering. As I approached a pass where the trail curved around to attain the Northeast Face, the wind and graupel smacked me with emphasis. I was forced to retrieve my short ice tools for support and sort of crabbed along. If I'd tried to walk upright, the hurricane-force wind would've blown me over. I crabbed around to the Face and was shocked to see headlamps all over the bloody place. I wasn't the only one who was taking advantage of the iced-up conditions.

There's a tiny stone hut at the base from which a stream of climbers emanated. There were also several tents. I'll give it to the United Kingdom climbers; they're a hearty lot. At least one party climbed on every route worth climbing on the mountain, with queues on the more classic or easy routes. I was feeling awful regardless, so I headed back down and slept most of the day.

I now knew the Face was in great *nick* (condition), however. I'd gone up on a Sunday, which was a mistake. So, Monday morning I got up at three a.m., ate some miserable gruel, took my oxy and cold medication, and headed back up. The sheep were still hunkered down, but the wind wasn't quite as brutal as the previous day. The entire upper mountain was in cloud. I hiked around to the Face, and saw a few headlamps, but not nearly as many as the previous day. And there were none on Tower Ridge. This is one of the longest rock routes in Scotland. It's highly exposed, with good solid rock, and wildly scenic. A true classic.

Not much dry rock for me, though. The ridge was plastered with rime in most places, more than a foot thick at times, as well as patches of iced rock, frozen turf, and hard snow. I ran up to the base of the ridge, harnessed up, and took off. I'd never experienced anything like rime climbing. It was like climbing on Styrofoam. It probably helped that I couldn't see more than ten feet ahead of me, due to the howling whiteout with shotgunned snow and graupel. I couldn't see the appalling sweep of icy rock above me. This was what Scots climbers sportingly call "full conditions," or "a bit fresh."

I attained the summit without incident after a couple of hours. I couldn't see a damn thing but wandered around and examined an old rime-encrusted observatory. The beta warns about wandering around. A number of people who have hiked up the dog route have fallen off the Northeast Face. How they fell off is a mystery. Large and obvious warning posts are planted along the edge, which appear to have been there for decades. Perhaps the hikers are blown off, which is entirely possible. I hiked down the long dog route trail, grinning with delight and relief, drove back, and fell into bed. I saw nobody else from the time I started on the ridge to the parking lot.

It was a revelatory experience. Nobody knew the specifics of where I was climbing, and rescue was impossible in those conditions. It doesn't get much worse than "a bit fresh," at least at low altitudes. Safely and rapidly climbing while maintaining a flow state through such conditions made it seem as if I'd crossed a critical mental threshold.

Soloing Tower Ridge in full Scottish conditions slammed me through a mountainous meteorological door.

Linda and I later explored the Scottish hills in what's sportingly called "summer," as a prelude to me working another stint in England. As in winter, the main challenge was the weather. We arrived in the very maw of what even the Scots referred to as the worst September in a long time. Earlier summer isn't advisable due to pervasive thick clouds of *midgies*, or biting gnats, making many areas intolerable.

The Highland weather forecasts included creative and hopeful predictions such as "largely cloudy, with occasional bursts of sun" or "dry, with mist and fog." We would've been sitting around an awful lot if we'd wanted to climb hard rock routes. A consistent pattern of gales pummeled us the entire time. The wind speed on the summits was sixty miles per hour on average and much higher at times. It was often impossible to walk without a trekking pole. I held a pole by its strap as a test. If the pole blew out horizontally, it was bloody fresh. I sometimes donned my sunglasses because horizontal rain, sleet, and graupel—in a few cases *angling up*—stung my eyes and impaired my vison.

An older gentleman we met in a bunkhouse chided me in the midst of a meteorological bitch session. "Surely you dinna come to Scotland for the weather?" Good point, brother. Despite the driving precipitation and screaming wind, Linda and I climbed over a dozen peaks.

On the Isle of Skye, we climbed the east ridge of the northernmost peak of the Black Cuillin range, Sgurr nan Gillian. We wanted to reconnoiter a traverse of the entire range. A couple who were descending as we approached voiced dire warnings about the wind. They turned back, complaining, "it's dangerous up there!" Sigh. It's a mountain, they're all dangerous. Several other parties bailed on the route due to the wind. Needless to say, Linda and I continued.

A weird event, perhaps even unprecedented in the history of mountaineering, occurred. The approach is over slimy boulders, and I slipped due to a blast of wind. That's why I carry a trekking pole. However, as I lurched forward, the tip of the pole caught on a rock, slipped, whipped back and slapped me across the face. Intense pain, subsequent swelling, and a black eye resulted, which caused people to avoid me, thinking I was a rough bloke. Thankfully, I experienced no loss of vision. Needless to say, we continued. We were glad we brought a rope for the purpose of simul-climbing and avoidance of wind-related dislodgement from the ridge. The rock was superb, rough and solid, and we summited in pelting rain, with no further issues.

Although we planned to traverse the entire Black Cuillin the next summery day, the forecast was more than a bit fresh: hundred mile-per-hour winds on the summits and snow down to 2,000 feet. Strangely, the Black Cuillin is owned by the Clan MacLeod. As in the Russell Mulcahy movie *Highlander*, for us "there could only be one" summit. We bailed and headed elsewhere. Those who go to Scotland definitely dinna go for the weather.

In 2007, to celebrate my fifty years of life and twenty years of marriage, Linda and I girded ourselves for the long flight and spent five weeks climbing and hiking in New Zealand. An initial risk was embarrassment. We rented a Wicked Camper in Christchurch. These discount rental vehicles were mostly 1990s Toyota minivans outfitted for camping, and painted in various original graphic displays. Some were cool, like a Simpsons theme, and tributes to musicians such as Jimi Hendrix and the Beatles. Part of the Wicked experience, though, was a lack of theme choice. By luck of the draw, we ended up with the *Junkwaffel* van, which sported a couple of cartoonishly wicked ladies, and a weird lizard-like creature leering at them and exclaiming *Yum!* The kind offer, *I'm No Gynecologist, but I'll Take a Look,* was emblazoned on the rear. Could've been worse, as we could've been assigned the *The Sex Police* van, which ordered other drivers and passersby to *Spread 'Em!*

We wanted to climb Mt. Cook—Linda's surname, which now goes by the Maori name Aoraki. This is a giant peak with an appearance and scale similar to Mt. Waddington in the British Columbia Coast Range, and amusingly a Linda Glacier cascades down it. Unfortunately, the typical Linda Glacier descent route wasn't negotiable due to large open crevasses. It was also late in the austral summer, and the snowpack was low and the temperature high. Indeed, the mountain guides weren't guiding Mt. Cook at all, and there had been recent fatalities from rockfall.

It may have been possible to climb the mountain via another route and descend the other side, but this introduced logistical and physical difficulties—physical in the sense of having to climb and carry-over the peak with an overnight pack. Linda had developed exercise-induced arthritis in her shoulder and was limited in terms of how much weight she could carry, so this wasn't feasible. Any route on the mountain would've been dangerous unless we climbed and descended in the dark.

I told a young woman who was working at the Mt. Cook hostel that we were considering climbing Mt. Cook. She seemed outraged, and cried, "You can't just climb Mt. Cook!"

I asked, "Are there restrictions or something?"

She replied, "No, but you Americans come here thinking just because it's less than 4,000 meters it's easy. You need to hire a guide."

I couldn't resist replying, "But, I'm Canadian, and I've been climbing longer than you've been alive," which didn't help matters.

We learned later there had been numerous recent rescues of American climbers, so those events may have provided a basis for her surly attitude.

As a consolation prize, we headed west to climb the north ridge of Mt. Tasman or Horokoau, the second highest peak in New Zealand. One nonintuitive aspect was directional. It took me a while to get it in my head north in the southern hemisphere is the direction of the sun at noon. As I take pride in being able to navigate *sans* instruments, this was a little disconcerting at first.

Hiking to the Pioneer Hut near the peak wasn't a safe or reasonable option, due to the heavily crevassed lower glaciers and adjoining heavily bushed ridges. So, we saddled up and flew. Starting out in a warm coastal subtropical forest zone and getting dropped off fifteen minutes later on a blinding glacier with big peaks all around was just weird. Given there were so many helicopters buzzing around New Zealand with no apparent air traffic control, our arrival was a relief from an aerial risk perspective.

The sun was more intense than we'd ever experienced due to the extensive Southern Hemisphere ozone hole at the time, the altitude, and the reflective snow. We fried our noses despite careful use of hats and heavy sunblock. I couldn't identify a consistent weird and foul smell in the hut until I realized *the insides* of my nostrils were burned from the blazing snow. We bought thin but fashionable scarves after this for facial protection, which made us feel quite French.

We started walking at four a.m. across a mile or so of glacier, then up through a large icefall containing, as one hut dude put it, "the mother of all crevasses." Some of these monsters could swallow a yacht, or an entire team of climbers. Linda and I were alone on the mountain. Fortunately, there were intact snow bridges the whole way. A mist of snow rolled in, and the route was whited out at times. The climbing in general was straightforward, but tenuous as it was largely crappy snow and *snoice*, with little true ice. From the summit more than 3,000 feet above the hut, the views of Mt. Cook and surroundings were wondrous. We could see the ocean on either side, and we could see Mt. Cook was indeed out of the question for the season. Sixteen hours later, we arrived back at the hut. A superb alpine climb, one of the best we've ever climbed. I'm glad in a sense Mt. Cook was out of condition, otherwise we probably wouldn't have climbed this route.

We climbed other peaks without incident, but an exception was a *couloir* (gully) ice route on the south face of Mt. Haast. The ice wasn't the greatest. I wasn't confident in the holding power of screws, so I soloed the leads. I also knocked off a lot of ice, and despite good placement of belays, I managed to hit Linda on her arthritic shoulder with a dinner plate of ice falling more than a hundred feet. She screamed in pain, but I needed to complete the pitch in order to get in good pro. After a rest, she was able to climb, and we completed the couloir. She's a tough lady.

Our friend Adam was keen to climb in South America. Linda wasn't interested in climbing, but went along to hike. We thought about Peru, which is easier in a logistic sense as it's more touristed. The bigger peaks in Peru, however, have become more dangerous recently due to glacial recession. The Bolivian peaks seemed safer.

Traveling in Bolivia was risky in terms of getting around efficiently, especially as English is a third or fourth or nonexistent language, and we were all marginal Spanish-speakers. We hired a Bolivian mountain guide to organize the trip, but not to guide us on climbs. He was the only Bolivian at the time to have summited Everest, a national hero who appeared on not one, but three postage stamps. He seemed to be friends with everybody in Bolivia. We scored many free pisco sours in restaurants. Another risk was the Bolivian government's unfriendliness to Americans at the time due to the "war on drugs." We traveled on our Canadian passports.

Altitude was the major issue in Bolivia. The airport, located in the slum of El Alto outside La Paz, is over 13,000 feet. We started taking acetazolamide (Diamox) beforehand. Initially, we experienced no physiological problems other than choking on dense clouds of diesel fumes in the cities. We were told coca helped adjust to the altitude, but coca leaves, which were legal, had no effect on me. Cocaine, which wasn't legal, had an effect on me back in the day, but I wasn't going to go there. We didn't observe many people aside from taxi drivers chewing coca, although coca tea was widely available, including in hotel lobbies.

We heard travel myths and misperceptions. One myth warned of ubiquitous packs of mean, rabid dogs. Every dog we encountered, and they were everywhere except in central La Paz, was either friendly or indifferent. Good thing we didn't go for the prophylactic rabies shots. And where were the pickpockets? I never felt a hand get even close; it would've been smacked hard otherwise. Maybe we weren't travelling in sketchy areas, after all. We observed no spitting llamas. Perhaps they didn't have sufficient chaw?

The best myth, though, was promoted by the El Presidente at the time, who proclaimed excessive chicken consumption turned straight men gay. This was due to an incorrect interpretation of growth-hormone effects. Linda and I were vegetarians at the time, so I wasn't at risk. But was I? It was difficult traveling as a vegetarian in Bolivia, and despite our frequent warnings of *vegetariano*, we belatedly discovered our supposed vegetarian soup had been boiled with chicken or other meat, with the meat removed afterward. This contributed to constant gastrointestinal issues.

I took three courses of ciprofloxacin to treat infections due to fecal contamination of food or water, and lost over ten pounds over the course of a month. Those who make frequent climbing trips to developing countries must have guts of stainless steel.

After acclimatization at the stupendous Lake Titicaca, we geared up for the Condoriri Valley, a lovely area with relatively low-elevation peaks of less than 19,000 feet. Having our stuff transported for us and hauled up to base camp on burros was luxurious. What respectable beasts, except for one obnoxious male who tossed his load multiple times. Our gear was undamaged despite this behavior. Later, he displayed his impressive erect burro-hood to Adam and me every time we looked his way. "What d'y'all think about this?" he seemed to say. He didn't appear to be interested in Linda.

The *arrieros*, or handlers, were all women. We were humbled by the rural Bolivians' strength and endurance. The load that Randy-Ass had dumped weighed over sixty pounds, and a nice little lady just whipped it back up on his back with no problem. We pranced about with our lightweight day packs and foppish climbing clothing costing more than a year's worth of Bolivian wages. This started to bother me by the end of the trip. Our White, rich-country privilege was obvious.

Our base camp was over 15,000 feet, already beating Linda's and my previous altitude record of 14,000-plus. I was concerned about Linda's safety.

She was hiking around while Adam and I climbed, so I encouraged her to carry an ice ax and a radio. Considering she was larger than the average Bolivian male, this strategy was likely overkill. She fell asleep once in a meadow and awoke surrounded by spitless llamas gazing down at her.

None of the peaks Adam and I climbed were challenging in a technical sense, but despite acetazolamide and a period of acclimation, I was sucking wind like a sprinter much of the time. I was plenty fit, but never did fully acclimate to the higher altitudes. Linda had no problem at all, and Adam was in-between. My lack of acclimation was irritating. I knew if a particular peak had been 14,000 feet or lower, I would've been skipping up the thing. I don't have a big barrel chest, and no matter how rapidly and deeply I inhaled, it just wasn't enough. Constant gastrointestinal illness didn't help either. I was just wiped out. Regardless, we summited several fine peaks from the valley.

The larger peak Huayna Potosi exceeds 6,000 meters or just shy of 20,000 feet, for those of a goal-seeking inclination. An alternative name is Caca Aca. *Like, dude, we rocked Titicaca and Caca Aca, while chawing coca.* Caca Aca is above a valley reminiscent of old mining Superfund sites in Montana and Idaho. Silver and gold mining have been the toxic death of many Bolivian waterbodies, including the foul sewer that used to be a river running under La Paz. This valley is a prime example, with massive mine tailing mounds everywhere. If we blocked this devastation out, though, Caca was an amazing mountain.

No burros this time—the approach to the high camp was rocky scrambling—but we employed human porters. It snowed the previous week, and the exposed approach was icy. One porter was having trouble due to his worn-out sneakers, so Adam helped him with his load. A German climber offered unhelpful advice, "Careful, this is dangerous!" Wish I'd known German for, "Sir, I'm sure you realize all mountains are dangerous?"

We heard some parties start out climbing at midnight, which seemed unbelievable until somebody explained many of the local guides like to be back in La Paz by lunchtime. It was daft in terms of the length of the tropical day; the sun rises at six and sets at six, so these folks are getting to the summit before sunrise. Indeed, several parties tramped by and woke us with their jabbering at about one a.m. Adam and I were lazy and slept in until three or so. Unfortunately, we climbed under a band of loose rock just in time for some of the early descenders to drop a substantial boulder past us.

We also observed many guided but flailing *Lonely Planeteer* climbers. The Bolivian guidebook proclaimed this 6,000-meter peak as "suitable for beginners." Maybe the authors took their cue from *Selected Sandbags*. The results were failed attempts, collapsed climbers, puke, crap, and so on scattered along the trail. Worse, some of the so-called guides didn't appear to be familiar with basic glacier travel, such as keeping a tight rope between individuals so if one partner falls in a hole, the others can self-arrest quickly and stop his fall. That caca-show ranked up there with the worst of the Alps and Colorado.

After the industrial and *tourista* experience of Huyana Potosi, I wasn't sure what to expect of Illimani, the tallest peak in Bolivia. At least we didn't have to drive through El Alto and pollute our lungs again. The drive was rough but fascinating, bouncing through the Cañon de Palca, which was reminiscent of the Utah canyon country. The road weaved through appalling cliffs with no guardrails, and we were in a tippy Land Rover with hundreds of pounds of bodies and equipment stuffed into it. Nido de Condores was the 17,000-foot high camp. Sadly, no condors. All the climbers probably scared them away.

Two porters hauled up eighty-pound loads to this camp in sacks, wearing the usual sandals. The approach was exposed and loose scrambling in places, so this feat was even more impressive. The camp itself was in a spectacular location, with a view of glaciers and calving seracs on both sides of the ridge. Crapping was a little perilous, requiring climbers to hang their butts out over a nasty-ass cliff. Due to our gastrointestinal issues, this wasn't a trivial concern.

We started climbing the peak the next morning, but Adam suffered severe gut issues. We bailed soon after embarking from camp. He felt fine later in the day after resting and taking more cipro, so we gave it a go the next morning. We were treated to a wondrous scene of Illimani's shadow on the terminator line before sunrise. The peak looked deceptively easy, but we ended up running three pitches on one icy section.

It was also quite cold. Halfway up, Adam asked if I was okay. I was sucking wind, lips numb from the cold, and had copious snot streaming from my nose. I mumbled something incomprehensible. He asked, "You're not getting wobbly on me, are you?" to which I blubbered, "Node, I'b nod; I'b fahn." This was good enough for him, as he carried on, and we reached the transcendent summit with jungle clouds far below. We were entirely alone on the route and summit.

Despite the facts this was a great trip and Adam and I summited multiple peaks up to 21,122 feet, I suffered continual gastrointestinal illness and didn't acclimate well. I don't plan to climb or trek in such a country again or go to such a high altitude, except maybe in a jet. I have great respect for climbers who drag themselves up peaks of this elevation and higher, but the physiological door to international high-altitude mountaineering shut me out.

Also, being relatively wealthy in an economically poor country felt uncomfortable. I suppose climbers from wealthy countries who travel to mountaineering areas such as South America and Asia on a frequent basis ignore the wealth disparities. There's little they can do about it aside from paying the locals decent wages. I just didn't feel a burning desire to climb high mountains. There were plenty of perilous, lower elevation doors to enter.

We traveled to Hawaii once from Canada and, like many tourists, snorkeled, body surfed, and such. We hiked up the huge Mauna Kea on the Big Island. Most importantly from a risk perspective, Kilauea was erupting. We were told that it was worthwhile to hike across a few miles of recent lava at sunset to observe flowing lava up close in the darkness. This was before the National Park Service disallowed this sort of thing. We parked at the end of the highway where a large flow had buried the village of Kalapana and started hiking across the black *pahoehoe,* or smooth solidified lava.

It became dicey as we approached the molten lava flows. We were never quite sure whether the solid lava we treaded upon was molten underneath. A barbecued foot would result if we punched through. Regardless, the flowing lava was truly trippy, as long as the wind blew away rather than toward us; the latter resulting in a blast furnace effect. The lava flowing into the ocean created giant clouds of steam. We were highly amused that the only other party out there was a group of three Canadians. We joked with them that only Canadians were crazy enough to be doing this.

The other Canadians left before sunset. Linda and I hung out for a few hours, until it was pitch-dark, longer than we should've. No moon shone, it was cloudy, and we were in the middle of miles of black lava, miles from any lights. Once we left the glowing lava streams, it was as dark as it gets. And I'd forgotten to replace the batteries in the one headlamp we carried. About halfway back, it failed. We could hear waves, but we knew we didn't want to get too close to the sound or we'd fall off a cliff into the ocean. So, we paralleled the coast, gingerly picking our way across the convoluted terrain. Neither of us tripped and fell, which was good as the lava was glassy and would've shredded us. Eventually, we could see a dim light in a little shack at the end of the road. After this experience, I made damn sure to replace headlamp batteries before any hike or climb, and to carry spares.

The opposite of fire, of course, is ice; a dangerous door indeed.

One of the few solid sections on Mt. Blane, Alberta. The bullet holes in my helmet are fake (credit: J. Boyce).

"Look ma, no hands!" The risk scientist on the huge limestone slabs of Ha Ling Peak, Alberta. I previously took a whipper on this route (credit: J. Boyce).

Linda descending the lower ridge of Mt. Selwyn, Alberta, for the long trek back to the hut after the rap anchor failed and she went a-flying (credit: R. C. Lee).

Linda rapping over the 'schrund of AA (Athabasca-Andromeda) Glacier, after summiting Mt. Andromeda, Alberta. I was hit in the helmeted head by a substantial rock while setting up the anchor for this rap (credit: R. C. Lee).

Linda and my left foot on an early morning jaunt, huffing up the icy Kain Face of Mt. Robson, British Columbia. My foot is in this position because it's tiring to rely on those front crampon points stuck into the ice. So, I avoided it when possible (credit: R. C. Lee).

(above) Putting off shoveling out the tent by taking photos of typical whiteout conditions on the Columbia Icefields, Alberta. One of our partners fell into a crevasse while skiing down from this camp (credit: R. C. Lee).

(right) Scary hair on Mt. Athabasca, Alberta. Sign of an imminent lightning strike, yet Linda's happy to be there. Immediately after I took this photo we hauled ass down the hill (credit: R. C. Lee).

The happy couple alone on the spectacular summit of Mt. Sir Donald, British Columbia. We bailed from our first attempt due to crowding. Note that we didn't wear wedding rings for our many years of climbing, as they would have become horribly scratched (credit: R. C. Lee).

Linda lochan, stochan, and barrelan up the Northeast Ridge of Sgor an Lochan Uaine, Scotland, in high winds and horizontal rain (credit: R. C. Lee).

Linda paying homage to the great Mt. Tasman, New Zealand, with Mt. Lendenfeld in the background. She's actually removing a snow picket used for running pro (credit: R. C. Lee).

"Ugh, dude, I don't feel so good, eh." I'm ill from bacteria and altitude in the Condoriri Valley in Bolivia, but still climbing (credit: A. Beardmore).

Caca-show on Huayna Potosi, Bolivia. Note the loose rope between members of the lower team, which is a no-no. In fact, there is no reason to even wear a rope at this point, as all of the crevasses are visible. The upper climber (perhaps a Lonely Planeteer) is exhausted or sick to the point of collapse. If I'd anticipated that I would write a risky memoir, I would've taken more photos of this type over the years (credit: R. C. Lee).

The Ice Door

WE'RE CLIMBING A FROZEN WATERFALL HUNDREDS OF FEET TALL, WITH wicked, yards-long ice daggers hanging over our heads, dripping frigid water. The temperature is around zero Fahrenheit. We climb almost vertical to over-hanging ice as fast as possible with two ice hammers in our hands and crampons on our feet, held onto the ice by perhaps a half-inch of metal hit or kicked into the ice, maintaining two or three points of contact at all times. As a leader, I'm making continuous decisions as to whether I should just keep moving, or hang and place screws that may or may not hold a fall. I seriously don't want to get a case of shaking jimmy-legs from fatigue. In places, the ice is so thin, screws are useless. I know that I simply can't fall. The ice can collapse on us, and an ava-lanche from above can wipe us off the route. Ice climbing is a heavily guarded door, but we hack our way through it and are transformed.

❧

The Canadian Rockies are a world center for climbing frozen waterfalls. Non-climbers and even some climbers may think climbing water ice is an insane activity, but it was the most addictive thing Linda and I'd ever done. We climbed in a wild, tripped-out environment. The icy colors ranged from violet to blue to white, and even yellow. The formations ranged from nar-row pillars to broad walls. Some were reminiscent of icicles hanging from a roof, but on a massive scale. Sometimes you could see water running under thin ice. Many climbs formed in remote and unforgiving winter mountain wilderness.

The unknown was a major appeal. Even though we often carried guide-book descriptions or other beta, each climb felt like an adventure. It was thrilling to venture around the corner of a frozen stream bed after hiking in and witnessing a spectacular several-hundred-foot icy work of natural art cascading down a cliff. And we were nearly always alone. On ice, the climbing path was in large part one of your choosing, as opposed to rock, which dictates routes based on holds. This freedom was appealing.

We needed to maintain focus when it was cold, the wind howling, freezing water dripping in our faces. We could've been speared by ice daggers or sheared off by an avalanche. Psychologically, the most difficult challenge was not getting good foot and ice tool plants, or sticks. It was exhausting both physically and mentally. We were reduced to the primal objectives of not falling off, or not dying from other means, yet we spent enormous amounts of time, effort, and money to achieve these objectives.

There was no better way to forget about work. There was also no better way to train for hard alpine climbing. Ice climbing may be a nonintuitive door to a flow state, but it worked for us.

Rick, with whom I rock climbed a few times when Linda and I first moved to New Mexico, was ten years my senior, but he was an ex-Marine, an ultra-runner, and a much better rock climber than me. He'd climbed waterfall ice in an earlier era. We once discussed why we even climbed ice, when typically, we wanted to get it over with as soon as possible. He offered an astute and uniquely Vietnam-vet-ish perspective: "Think of it this way: You've led a hard pitch, you've set up a belay and tied in, and you can finally relax and enjoy life. Man, that great feeling is the closest I can get to heroin anymore." Perhaps part of this feeling is due to endorphin release, as ice climbing hurts.

Although Linda and I considered the rewards to be great, anybody who says ice climbing is *fun* hasn't done much of it or has only done it in ideal conditions. Or perhaps they have a perverse definition of fun, as opposed to going to a party, making love, or just hanging out at a mountain lake on a nice sunny day. It would be interesting to survey ice climbers with regard to the *fun* opinion. Maybe they're just better at ignoring the risk, misery, and pain than I ever was. It could be fun, but only for short bits of ice or time.

A particular ice climb morphed from year to year, depending on the amount of precipitation, temperature, and so on. Some ice climbs were frozen all year, but only in frigid areas such as the Columbia Icefields. Guidebook descriptions were general at best: describing the steepness and length, and in some cases how to get off.

When planning a climb the main criteria were whether the waterfall was frozen at all, driving and hiking conditions, how *fat* the climb was or how much ice was present, and the condition of the ice. We also climbed sections of rock with ice tools and crampons, which is easier than it sounds once we became comfortable with it.

The best ice was like climbing hard ice cream, with single-whack sticks the whole way up. On thin ice, we needed to be delicate and precise. Bad ice required digging to remove crappy layers and find good ice. I beat out holes several inches deep sometimes before finding good ice. Sometimes, I didn't find it. I've never cussed more in my life than on such ice, but cussin' never helped.

The more we hit and kicked the ice, the faster we fatigued. In my early ice days, I wore myself out on climbs until I watched a female mountain guide leading the classic pillar Carlsberg Column. I had an epiphany: I needed to climb like a girl. It's a lot more efficient and elegant. Of course, Linda naturally climbed like a girl.

If a pick became stuck in the ice, it was a real pain getting the tool out. With leash-less tools, knocking the thing out and dropping it was possible, and could be a death sentence. We used two hammer-headed tools. An ice ax adze on the non-pick side could cleave your face if the tool popped off in that direction. Hammers can cause enough damage.

Ropework on ice was arduous, but worse if the climb was wet and the ropes frozen. Pulling two, two-hundred-foot lengths of frozen nylon through a belay device was character building at best. Hauling rope was often the most tiring aspect of ice climbing, especially since Linda climbed fast, and she didn't like a slack rope. A common admonition was, "Take, goddamn it!" There's a good reason most Canadian Rockies mountain guides have burly arms.

A rope stuck on a rap due to freezing or wrapping itself around an icicle was a pain. This situation sometimes necessitated climbing back up to retrieve the rope after a rap. We avoided rapping when possible, but walking off was sometimes impossible or risky. Nothing quite compares to scrambling down steep, icy or snowy scree slopes with huge exposure in mountain boots and crampons. We therefore became expert at placing rap stations.

Pro was another issue. Modern ice screws are hollow, precision machined, and have sharp teeth so they can be screwed as rapidly as possible into the ice. Speed was important, because placing a screw on a vertical section involved hanging on one tool and your crampon points. No matter how good the screwing technique, it was tiring. Unless there were numerous convenient ledges, we would forego trying to use too many screws. The best pro was sometimes in rock, not ice. Depending on the climb, we might be carrying rock pro in addition to ice screws. This meant even more weight to haul up a climb.

The strength of a screw was dependent on the quality of the ice. There was no point in putting a screw in bad or thin ice. It wouldn't hold a fall anyway. Even on good ice, we often clipped *screamers* on the screws most subject to a hard fall. Screamers are slings sewn in an accordion fashion to themselves with stitches designed to give way. They rip out lengthwise to a full-strength sling, limiting the load on the screw in the event of a hard fall.

Canada and other ice climbing destinations were bloody cold in the winter. Linda and I soon learned it was difficult to stay warm if we belayed when the temperature fell much below zero degrees Fahrenheit or twenty below zero Celsius. We rarely carried insulated *puff daddy* jackets to wear while belaying; rather, we just hiked and climbed as fast as we could so we could get back into a warm vehicle as soon as possible. I soloed climbs and we both climbed easy routes when the temperature was colder than zero degrees Fahrenheit, but only because we could move continuously and thus stay warm. We often climbed in underwear and outer clothing featuring *round the world* zippers, which allowed us to perform excretory business without having to take our harnesses or pants off.

Maintaining blood flow in our hands was the main issue. We couldn't wear mittens or thick gloves while technical ice climbing. We had to manipulate tools, rope, and pro. Our hands were also above our heads much of the time, gravity draining the blood out of them. Initially we used straight-shaft tools, which we needed to grip hard, and leashes, which tended to restrict circulation and make our hands even colder. The advent of leash-less tools with nice handles allowed us to clip a tool to a harness, in order to shake our hands to increase blood flow. They were a godsend. Disposable chemical handwarmers worn inside thin gloves also helped.

The *screaming barfies* was an excruciating condition that resulted when blood flowed back into cold, blood-deprived hands. The barfies amounted to an extreme case of the tingling gwenders. We were gwendered often, and screamed a few times, but never barfed.

The risk of injuring or killing a second climber was always present. It was crucial to set up belays so the second climber was out of the line of fire. Unlike rock climbs, where we only released a lot of rock if we were, well, in the Canadian Rockies, releasing ice was the norm unless we were fortunate to be climbing high quality ice. We had to be creative in terms of setting up belays. Sometimes, bombing the second climber was unavoidable. They hid under their helmet and pack and hoped for the best.

Good and consistent communication with the second climber was crucial as well. Even if Linda and I weren't wearing a toque and hood under or over our helmets, it was difficult to hear each other due to wind, dripping water, and so on. Some people tried various signaling techniques like pulling on the rope three times, but this always seemed silly to us. Instead, we just used lightweight radios. Instead of yelling at the top of our lungs ("Linda, blah blah!" "*Whaaat?*" "*Blaaah blaaah, dammit!*"), or jerking on the rope and hoping your partner remembered the patterns, we just conversed using our compact radios. Technology is sometimes wonderful. I'm confounded more people don't use radios, even in sport climbing. Once small, lightweight units were developed, we used them for any kind of roped climbing. Now days, they only weigh a few ounces.

Valley side slopes on approaches to climbs could avalanche, as could snow slopes above the ice. National Park staff bombed wind-loaded avalanche bowls above a few popular climbs on a routine basis, so climbers weren't wiped out from above. We were never hit by a substantial slide, but we were as careful as possible when assessing the joint risk of a particular climb's terrain, location, and the general avalanche risk level.

Linda and I once arrived at the base of the climb Bourgeau Right-Hand near Banff to find debris from a small slide, including the mangled body of a mountain goat. Goats are mountain experts; they live there for godssake. It made us consider proceeding even more carefully. Was this the entirety of the slide or was it just foreplay to a larger one? Bourgeau is an oft-bombed climb, but it hadn't been blown yet that season. We said screw it, drove back to Canmore, and enjoyed a nice coffee.

A typical ice climb involved: getting up early in Calgary or staying in a hotel or hut, driving to the climb, hiking or skiing in carrying a pack with thirty or forty pounds of ropes, pro, and so on, getting fueled, watered, and geared up as quickly as possible due to the cold, launching up into the unknown and often the unknown coming back down, hiking or skiing out, and driving back home as soon as possible.

At the time, I weighed about one-eighty-five, which was as skinny as I could be and still maintain the strength required to climb. The typical gross weight of me and my gear while leading with a small pack was well over two-hundred pounds. Carrying much more up an ice climb would've been just arduous. I suppose I could've worked on getting stronger, but this seemed too much like work.

I admire people who train and go to gyms, but this was never something I could force myself to do. I preferred to just climb. Linda and I climbed a lot, plus dog runnies and yoga. We were plenty fit in a cardio sense. My main method for monitoring my cardio state on an approach or climb was noticing if my eyeballs started pulsing. If so, I'd slow down and concentrate on breathing. The closest I came to strength training was hanging a couple of ice tools from the beams in the basement and doing pullups with them every night until I got bored with it. Linda didn't even do this. Perhaps she had better technique than me.

We were fortunate to live in Calgary during a time when ice climb-ing was less common than it is now. We could observe, climb with, and learn from some of the best ice and mixed climbers in the world. Many of these Canadians would be world-famous if they were interested in self-promotion, but they just loved to climb or work in the mountains. Access to the climbing culture was invaluable. It was similar to playing music in

Chapel Hill in the 1980s. Whether ice climbing or playing music, hanging with people who were much better than me was inspiring. We found a tribe of sorts.

The more Linda and I climbed, the more expertise we gained, but the greater the cumulative risk. We took things slowly at first, *top-roping* single pitches (setting up a doubled rope on an anchor at the top of a climb or belaying from above), then leading single pitches.

The first multi-pitch waterfall Linda and I climbed was Cascade Falls outside Banff, a relatively easy, thousand-foot climb. Cascade has probably killed more ice climbers in the Rockies than any other. This is due to its visibility from the highway, its technical ease and thus popularity, its south-facing aspect, and the huge avalanche bowl sitting above it. We climbed the route and descended in the early morning darkness, to minimize risk.

We became hooked on multi-pitch ice, and climbed between the pillars of an icy door.

I soloed many ice climbs. In most, but not all cases, I'd solo waterfalls Linda and I'd both previously climbed. At least I knew what I was getting into, including the descent. Leading on thin ice with no pro was the same risk as soloing. There was nothing to catch me if I fell. On easier and longer climbs, I'd often lead without pro to a belay, then bring Linda up on a rope I'd dragged behind me. Soloing or leading without pro was much faster and less tiring than placing pro, and I didn't have to carry as much weight.

Linda and I climbed This House of Sky in the Ghost River area using this technique. We climbed the ice, scrambled to the high ridge above, descended the ice climb French Technique in the adjoining canyon, and hiked back to the truck. This was a six-hour journey by ourselves on over a thousand vertical yards of ice in an astounding remote alpine wilderness.

Soloing was risky, but there were tense moments climbing with a roped partner. The amazing Polar Circus consists of 2,300 feet of climbing and over 1,600 feet of waterfall ice over nine or more technical pitches. It's one of the longest water ice climbs in the world, and it starts right next to the Icefields Parkway. Therefore, the climb often has more than one party on it when it's formed and fat.

The first time Linda and I attempted the climb, a party of Italians was ahead of us. On a runout way above my last pro on one of the steep middle pitches, I was bombed with an avalanche of climber-released snow and ice. I was reluctant to let go of one of my tools to get a screw in. I'm not sure how long I hung there, but it seemed like hours, and this situation was probably the only time I came close to falling from simple fatigue. Getting pummeled with countless chunks of snow and ice didn't help. I tried yelling up at the Italians, but who knew if they could understand me anyway. Eventually the barrage lightened and I was able to get a screw in. This was just damn dangerous, so I set up a rap and we bailed.

We returned and completed the climb at a later date. This was an instance when I led all the pitches without pro, except the final, partially overhanging pitch, to speed things up and stay ahead of another party behind us. Fortunately, we were able to do so. We *simul-rapped* the descent by simultaneously rapping off the same bolt anchors to save time. We had to descend the 2,300 feet quickly to get down before dark in midwinter. It took us seven hours of moving continuously on this huge climb to get up from and down to the car.

Wearing eyeglasses presented an unusual risk. Normally, we appreciated glasses because they helped guard our delicate eyeballs from flying ice shards. More importantly, we could see more clearly with them; Linda and I were both myopic. However, if the climb was steep and wet, glasses made seeing difficult. The climb that put my myopia into the past tense was called Lady Killer. We climbed it early season, which meant the Lady was dripping wet, yet the air temperature was cold. Our ropes, clothes, and everything else became coated in ice, including my glasses. I resorted to looking over them, with a focal point of less than a foot, to try and climb. It was ridiculously risky, and threatened to kill this dude, if not his lady.

For some reason, I could never tolerate contact lenses. I tried a few times, but the contacts at the time felt like rocks in my eyes. Coincidentally, when we returned to Calgary from this climb, a LASIK clinic was having a two-eyes-for-one surgery sale. A risk scientist by then, I asked the surgeon what his failure rate was.

He replied, somewhat huffily, "What do you mean?"

"How many surgeries have you done, and how many have resulted in uncorrectable eye damage?"

He was honest, telling me his failure rate was about one in a thousand, which was quite good, especially considering these were the early days of LASIK. He also revealed none of his other patients ever asked this question, which was shocking.

I made the risk-risk tradeoff between frozen glasses and the surgery and let him cut and zap my valuable eyes. I was unprepared for the sulfurous burning-hair odor. When I mentioned this, the surgeon noted in a jocular fashion, this being Cowtown Calgary and all, that some of his patients likened the odor to the stink of cattle branding. The first few times I felt raindrops and snowflakes on my LASIK-ed eyeballs were wondrous. I'd worn glasses since the third grade.

I didn't have my eyes burned for cosmetic reasons; glasses made me look smarter and accepting a low probability of permanent eye damage for the sake of vanity would've been crazy. Ice climbing wasn't the only reason for the surgery. Fogging of glasses under ski goggles was rather risky as well, especially in a whiteout on a glacier.

The surgery worked out well for me. Not all of my encounters with the medical system have resulted in injury. I know others for whom LASIK didn't work out so well, and they now have to live with the suboptimal results. After the surgery, I still tried to wear sunglasses or clear safety glasses to avoid the ice-chip-in-the-eye business, but if I was working hard and the temperature was cold, they fogged up, and went in the pack. Fortunately, my eyes were never punctured by ice chips.

☙

As a leader or soloing, a climber doesn't want to fall on ice because of the sharp objects in their hands and on their feet. I never fell as a second, and neither did Linda, so I don't know what risks exist in that situation. I wrote up my one consequential leader fall on ice on a Rockies climber's web-site, a new phenomenon at the time. Somebody submitted the account, unbeknown to me, to the American Alpine Club. They published it in the 2006 edition of *Accidents in North American Mountaineering*. I was startled when I browsed through the volume and started reading about myself.

The three-hundred-foot climb is called 2 Low 4 Zero. The guidebook states "most often 2 Low 4 Zero is an iced-up rock route, but it occasionally forms up fat." It was emaciated when we climbed it. The first pitch was mostly ice and seemed fine. We set up a bomber and protected belay for Linda. The second pitch was much thinner. I was doing okay, as I'd climbed a lot of thin ice and mixed ice and rock by then. I found some ice for a good screw, attaching this to one of the ropes with a screamer. I moved up and hooked my left tool on top of a sheet of ice five feet square and an inch thick and proceeded to make the next plant with my right tool.

The left tool pulled the entire ice sheet off the rock, and the hammer side of the tool popped me in the mouth, like Edward Norton punching himself in David Fincher's *Fight Club*. One of my incisors broke off and punctured my lip, but more importantly, I knocked myself off the climb. My feet were good, so this must have been a hammer blow of some force. I free-fell backward about ten or twelve feet, catching my right crampon on the ice and partially tearing the connective tissues in my ankle. I was wearing boots with a flexible upper, befitting mixed climbing. My leg may have broken with a stiff boot.

This fall produced enough force that it pulled Linda off her feet, but she and the pro held fast. I hung upside-down from a screw at a spot where the ice was a couple inches thick and separated from the rock. I grabbed the rope and pulled myself right side up. The first thing I pondered was the screw above me. It still looked good, and the screamer ripped out as intended. If this screw failed while I was monkeying around, I would've been truly screwed, so I monkeyed with a sense of urgency. I screwed in a *stubby* or short ice screw and tied into this, while Linda held me on belay. Meanwhile my ankle was hurting badly, and I was heavily bleeding from my mouth. I needed to set up a quick rap. There were no obvious cracks to place rock pro.

I drilled a sketchy *Abalakov* anchor in the thin separated ice, which is two intersecting holes in the ice through which a short length of cord is threaded and tied. Spitting blood, I drilled a stubby above this anchor as a backup. I pulled one rope through the screw above, set up the rap, spit out even more blood, hoped for the best, and rapped down. Linda rapped down from her belay using the other rope.

We had to walk out about three miles in the snow. The climb is in an area with several other good ice climbs and a trail was beaten out, otherwise this would've been much worse. Some kind climbers who happened to be on a nearby climb offered to run out for a rescue, but heaven forbid I'd consent to be rescued. Lovely Linda took most of the gear in her pack. I took our two ski poles for support, tightened my boot, and hobbled out. It was quite cold, which had contributed to the fall; the ice was brittle. But the cold helped manage the pain in my ankle.

Linda drove to the Canmore ER. I was examined, my facial wound glued shut, and my ankle X-rayed. I was sent on my way with a *be careful* or something nice but useless, and a recommendation for a dentist and physiotherapy. I finally felt like a proper Canadian male, as I was missing a front tooth, although not due to a hockey puck in the face. I suggested to the dentist I wanted a gold front tooth, but she ignored me. I'll rectify things when the present ceramic crown has to be replaced.

As an aside, when we first moved to Calgary, I asked a Canadian climber what he employed for home invasion or robbery management, as guns are much less common there compared to the US. His classic Canadian reply, "What do you think hockey sticks are for, eh?"

A great benefit of Calgary was the availability of excellent physiotherapy. I went to a clinic serving many pro and world-class amateur athletes, judging by the signed photos on the walls. They'd seen just about every sports-related injury possible. The ice soaks were inspiring, for example, but the real fun was in my sessions with the Marquis de Sade, a stocky bald guy who didn't care how much pain I was experiencing in my quest to jump back in the icy saddle. After only a couple of weeks, he ordered me to jump from a three-foot-high bench onto a small trampoline and back up, one-legged on the injured ankle.

He encouraged me with, "I've seen twelve-year-old girls do better than that, eh?" My reply to this was, "Fuck you, they don't weigh one-eighty-five, eh? Let's see you do it, fat ass." It was met with hearty gales of laughter. The Marquis and the other therapists were good at their jobs and accustomed to surliness on the part of athletes in pain.

Six weeks later, I was climbing again, albeit on steep climbs without long approaches, as walking on uneven terrain was painful for a while. Linda and I climbed Louise Falls near Lake Louise as a first day out, a relatively non-painful outing. It may have actually been preferable in the long-term to have broken my leg, as I now have a wobbly ankle.

In the *Accidents* report, I made the following statement: "Although I have done quite a bit of soloing on easy water ice, this experience has cured me of that. I would have surely died without a rope." It didn't take long for me to renege on the promise. I soloed the ice climb Massey's when it was thirty below zero, just to make sure my head was still in it. Sometimes it's just more efficient and safer to climb without pro and get it over with.

A cool dude who later climbed 2 Low 4 Zero and who heard about the incident contacted me and returned the screw I'd fallen on and left in the ice, as well as the ripped-out screamer. Cheers, bro! I still have the screamer, to remind me of the value of good pro and how close I came to augering. The gear worked as intended, but there's only so much that can be done to prevent incidents like this from happening in the first place, aside from not climbing. My tooth crown and loose ankle are also constant reminders.

A possibly unique injury in the annals of ice climbing occurred on a climb called Dream On, in a remote area of the Rockies foothills. The potential for injury existed even before the climb. On the approach hike, Adam and I had the choice of walking around a small frozen lake or walking a shorter path across it. We were slothful, so we chose the lake. We were confident with regard to the thickness of the ice, but being Canadian and accustomed to walking on sheets of ice, we didn't stop to put on crampons. Halfway across I briefly lost concentration and my legs flew up, and I went down on my back like a sack of potatoes. No problem, as I landed on my pack. Adam guffawed, so I was gratified when the same thing happened to him a few minutes later.

Adam always led when we climbed. He was better at leading than me, he liked to lead, and we often climbed more difficult routes compared to the ones I led with Linda. Adam's response when I once congratulated him on a tough lead was, "You didn't fall, so you could've led it." This may have been true, but occasionally being the second was a welcome relief for me.

We completed the climb, and Adam launched off on a bonus pitch. When he indicated I should follow, I moved up, but when I whacked the ice a shard flew out and hit my face. The ice shard was of a shape, trajectory, and velocity that it split my upper lip, directly below my nose, almost all the way through. It was a complete surprise, as on a typical ice climb, I was constantly showering my face with bits of ice. I've never heard of such an injury occurring to anybody else. It didn't hurt much, being cut by a piece of ice for godssake, but I was alarmed at the copious amount of blood pouring out of my lip.

I radioed to Adam and requested he lower me. When I reached a ledge, I packed snow on the wound. We then rapped down to the packs, he applied some butterfly strips to my split lip, and we headed out. I'd lost a lot of blood. The climb looked like a murder scene. Adam offered to call for a rescue, but I didn't think the injury was bad enough to warrant a helicopter and didn't want to ruin my no-rescue record, so we walked out.

Adam hauled butt to the Canmore ER and dropped me off. The attending doc gave me the bad news. Because the cut was smack in the middle of my upper lip, and the nerves wrap around from the spine to the front of the face, she needed to inject a numbing agent directly into the wound before stitching it up. I asked if she could give me a shot of whiskey and a bullet to bite, but she patiently smiled and offered a roll of gauze. I grabbed the sides of the bed, bit down on the gauze, and motioned to get it over with. Ten stitches later, I was released.

Linda and I were visiting Calgary from New Mexico. We'd moved by then, and we were staying with our friends Nick and Jean. Nick's a former speed skiing champion who has skied over one hundred and fifty miles per hour, and one of the funniest people we know. He seemed to consider it a challenge to keep me in stitches. I was forced to hold my upper lip together to avoid ripping stitches, and he was in stitches as a result. We were all just stitched up. The only long-term consequence is a scar on my upper lip, similar in appearance to a cleft palate scar.

Driving to climbs in the Canadian winter was sometimes challenging, although the main highways were well maintained. Black ice was a concern, so we needed to pay attention. When we moved to Calgary, we bought an all-wheel-drive Honda CRV and a set of studded tires. The rig was like a snowmobile, as long as the snow wasn't too deep. I enjoyed driving fast in snow and ice as long as I didn't have to worry about other drivers.

The Spray Lakes Road outside of Canmore, which was a deserted gravel highway in winter, was great fun. One of the first times I flew along this road in icy conditions back from a climb, I gently tapped the brakes on one of the few tight turns and the antilock braking system (ABS) engaged. This was a surprise; we had never previously owned a vehicle with this so-called safety feature. I'd never felt the need for it. It's designed for people who don't know how to control skids. I downshifted and there were no adverse consequences, but as soon as I got back, I called the dealer and asked if they could disable the ABS. I told them I didn't find it useful, and indeed considered it dangerous. After extensive discussion, including, "But sir, this is an important safety feature," I gathered that disabling the ABS wasn't an easy thing to do.

Airbags are a strange technology as well. It would be much safer for drivers to use four- or five-point suspension harnesses and to wear helmets, but the public would complain. Airbags can be risky in themselves and add to the cost of vehicles. I dread the safety implications of the coming days of self-driving cars.

A life-changing medical risk event occurred, perversely, when I was traveling from Calgary to present my research on medical errors at the annual Society for Risk Analysis conference in Baltimore, Maryland. My neck started to hurt on the plane, and by the time I reached the hotel, it felt like somebody was jolting me with an electric cattle prod. I thought perhaps it was an impinged nerve. I called Linda, and she suggested I call the concierge and ask if there was a massage therapist on call. I think the concierge was a little confused. He hesitated and replied, "Sir, I assume you would like a female, or we can make other arrangements?" I gathered they didn't have an actual therapist on call, as opposed to a masseuse who would give me a *happy ending*.

Meanwhile, the pain became much worse. I called a taxi and asked him to take me to Johns Hopkins. The taxi pulled up to what looked like an industrial loading dock in a bad 'hood, but there were numerous ambulances indicating the building was indeed the ER. I didn't know Johns Hopkins is one of the major draws for the best and brightest ER residents. They see a lot of inner-city trauma, and budding emergency docs and trauma surgeons love to see trauma.

It was a bad weekend night, even for Hopkins. A river of trauma cases flowed through triage, including gunshot wounds, knife wounds, fist-imposed wounds, sprains and broken bones from people slipping on ice; it went on and on. The waiting room was packed, in part because the weather was cold and homeless folk were coming in to get unfrozen. The ten or so cops in the waiting room escorted them out now and then to clear out space for patients. A shooting had occurred in the waiting room earlier in the day, so in addition to the ten cops, a guard in body armor toting an M-16 dourly surveyed the mayhem.

And I was there with a sore neck. I checked in and waited in a depressing sea of sick, injured, and homeless people. The only entertainment was a small TV playing the camp classic *Fire Down Below,* by Félix Enríquez Alcalá and starring Steven Seagal as a ridiculous pony-tailed EPA staffer who kicks ass. I suffered through most of the movie, trying to mask my pain with mirth, waiting more than an hour and a half as the pain worsened. By then a rash appeared, tracing my cervical C7 nerve from the hellish repository of awakened varicella zoster virus in my spine, up the left side of my neck and onto my face. I didn't know what it was, although shingles is common. I'd just never known anybody to suffer from it. Linda and now I call it *shinglers,* after the old Vincent Price horror movie *The Tingler.*

The pain progressed from electric cattle prod to red-hot electric cattle prod equipped with teeth like a weasel. It was unbelievably painful, and being a climber, I have a high pain tolerance. I decided to be more aggressive, so I grabbed the only unoccupied movable chair, sat in front of the triage nurse, and moaned with emphasis. She was manicuring her nails in the midst of the ER mayhem, but eventually asked, "Sir, what is your problem?" I replied, "I don't know, but on a pain scale of zero to ten, this is an eleven." She rolled her eyes, but then noticed the rash. She asked if I wanted to see a doctor. I thought, *No, I just want to weep and moan,* but I moaned an audible, "Yes."

Once I was triaged I lay in a bed suffering for at least half an hour before I got fed up, grabbed a nurse, and emphasized I *really* needed to be seen. A sleepy resident, probably on a twenty-hour shift, showed up an hour or so later and examined me.

"Oh, you have shingles. Do you want something for the pain?" he said. I thought, *No, I just want to suffer,* but I groaned, "Yes." He gave me some ibuprofen and acetaminophen, which did squat. He must have slept through pharmacology training. He then asked if I wanted an antiviral drug. I gave him a silent, *No, I just want to live with the pain,* but sighed, "Yes." He ordered the drug. Another half hour passed, no drug; I grabbed another nurse, and she said she'd look into it. Another half hour later the resident showed up and said, "Oh, you didn't get your antivirals." The faxed prescription had been lost, and the pharmacy never got it.

By the time I received the shot, it was too late to be effective, and I'd wasted several hundred dollars. I spent all night in an ER and came out worse than when I went in.

The end result of this escapade is permanent damage to my C7 nerve. Not only do I suffer chronic pain, but I have diminished function in my left arm and hand. Our Canadian primary care physician at the time ignorantly prescribed opioids for the neuralgia, which did nothing. We subsequently fired her. The Canadian health system is great, but some of the doctors aren't.

I take a drug called gabapentin (Neurontin) to mask the deep, cramping, itching pain in my neck. I'll take it the rest of my life unless nerve-regenerating technology is developed. I'm lucky it's reasonably non-toxic.

Around the same time, I also developed disc disease in the C4-C5 area. Neurologists disagree whether it's related to the neuralgia or not. My condition could also be related to poor posture, falling in our early skiing days and suffering whiplash, looking up a lot while climbing, or just getting old. The disc disease also causes pain and function issues, addressed by anti-inflammatories. For years, I popped ibuprofen and gabapentin every four or five hours in order to work and climb. Eventually I weaned myself off ibuprofen through chiropractic, physiotherapy, and yoga.

When climbing, I needed to take care with regard to logger's claw in my left hand, especially pulling rope. At least my hand cramped closed rather than flying open unexpectedly. Although my grip strength isn't truly affected, it feels like it is, which is disconcerting at times.

Side effects of gabapentin can include lack of coordination, dizziness, fatigue, and sleepiness. I take large doses to mask the pain. As a climbing test, after I'd taken the drug for a while, I soloed the thousand-foot Cascade Falls ice climb in an hour. I passed this test *sans* dying and went on with my climbing life. The only positive result of the neuralgia is a medical excuse to never wear a collared shirt and tie again. The feeling of most fabric on my neck drives me nuts.

I realized a likely culprit in the shinglers episode was stress. I was working too much, climbing too much, sleeping too little, and so on. Stress is a killer. It was a wake-up call. Something had to give. I cut back on travel, which was one of the less pleasant aspects of my job. It's just not worth the pain and suffering to be stressed, especially with regard to work. Of course, I didn't cut back on climbing at the time, but I became more aware of my physical limitations.

There was a possible disconnect between my professional development and my attitude toward risk while living in Canada. I became more knowledgeable, innovative, and adept in the scientific and applied fields of risk analysis and risk management. However, at the same time, Linda and I climbed harder and harder routes. In other words, I became more familiar intellectually with risk and the tradeoffs inherent in risk management, but I was voluntarily putting myself in riskier and riskier situations. I was also becoming more adept at climbing risk management, but this only goes so far with uncontrollable risks such as avalanches and rockfall. Risk is cumulative as well; the more I climbed, the more likely it was I'd be involved in a serious accident. I admit I was addicted to mountaineering and ice climbing. In order to maintain the same level of gratification, I needed to climb harder and harder.

We climbed most of our desired peaks and routes during our nine years in Calgary. A sore temptation existed to push the difficulty and risk ceiling higher and higher in order to climb more novel routes. Some climbers take this approach to the extreme and take the attitude, "We survived that one—let's climb something harder and more dangerous." Some never break this addiction, and it breaks them. Linda and I weren't that bad, but in ice and mixed alpine climbing, pushing the level of difficulty often meant we were dealing with situations where pro was sketchy or nonexistent. It was also difficult to become physically fitter without hanging out at climbing gyms or training by other means, which neither one of us had time or inclination to do. The same applied to mental fitness. In order to climb at a higher level, we would have had to climb more and harder.

Linda was also in a research rut at the University of Calgary. Coincidentally, she was recruited by the University of New Mexico (UNM). We hadn't planned to leave Canada, but they made her a professional offer she couldn't refuse. Indeed, UNM wanted Linda badly enough they created a position for me as *spousal baggage*. This was in the Department of Emergency Medicine.

We escaped the temptations and risks of the Canadian Rockies. However, when risks associated with other humans in the mountains are considered, which we rarely dealt with in the Canadian Rockies, the door to the American Rockies may have been more dangerous.

Old-school dry-tooling. I'm practicing mixed climbing on unnamed ice in David Thompson Country, Alberta, with straight-shaft tools and clunky plastic boots (credit: L. Cook)

I'm high off the deck taking out pro on the first pitch of the classic Wicked Wanda, in the Ghost River wilderness, Alberta (credit: A. Beardmore).

The American Rockies Door

THE FIRST COLORADO PEAK I CLIMB IS MT. SNEFFELS, AT 14,000-PLUS feet. I solo the Snake Couloir on the north side in early summer, when it's iced up. It's a long approach, so I backpack and camp in a flowery basin with no other humans around. The next morning, I climb the couloir alone with crampons and tools. As I approach the summit, I'm confused; I hear numerous voices. I'm shocked to see over a dozen people on the summit. Long queues of people are ascending and descending the dog route gully, which is easy but contains loose rock. None are wearing helmets, despite frequent hiker-released rockfall. There's a contingent of young, long-skirted women of some traditional religious affiliation wearing little lace caps to protect their valuable brain buckets from all the rocks whizzing past. Worse, I don't hear anybody bellowing "Rock!", the universal warning in the climbing world. Even worse, there's a huge thunderhead reminiscent of a nuclear mushroom cloud overhead, hidden from me until I summitted, yet there are people just starting to hike up. I've never seen anything like it. Rather than descend the crowded gully, I scramble as quickly as possible down an adjoining ridge, reach easier terrain, and run down the trail in my mountain boots to my tent on the north side. I barely avoid getting zapped or soaked. I begin my exit from the climbing world door.

Linda and I sold our Calgary home, cashed out our retirement accounts to avoid double-taxation, and moved to The Land of Enchantment. Sadly, we bought two homes, one in Albuquerque and one in Durango, Colorado, in 2007. The home in Durango was for mountain access.

Buying two homes in 2007 was a mistake, but who knew? We didn't, nor did nearly everybody else. Later, in discussing the mortgage crisis with a mathematician co-worker who had *quant* (financial modeler) friends on Wall Street, I realized how close we'd come to a true cascading economic disaster. Those guys cashed out retirement accounts and bought plane tickets to Costa Rica; it was that serious. In talking with many non-financial sector people, I don't think many Americans realized how close the US came to economic collapse. I was prepared to move back to Canada and made a list for packing the truck, which may or may not have been a good strategy. Thankfully, the federal government bank bailout prevented this disaster.

The main consequence for Linda and me was paying too much for two houses and suffering a substantial loss. This event caused us to pay more attention, inform ourselves, and plan more carefully with regard to financial risk.

The problem with large-scale financial risk is it's largely out of the control of individuals. Diversification of investments is often the only real individual risk management strategy available. Especially since the COVID-19 pandemic, Linda and I have little confidence the good ol' days of being able to plan ahead and rely on traditional means of financial planning will ever return, but there's little we can do about it. We manage the risks the best we can. A rational economic system would maximize individual wealth across the income spectrum, but we're not holding our breath. We haven't had much money most of our lives, and it won't kill us if it happens again.

At least Albuquerque is geologically stable, but similar to Seattle, *Quirky* has a big glowing nuke target on it. Our house is about three miles from a major nuclear warhead storage facility, as well as Sandia National Laboratory; whose primary mission is to develop weapons of mass destruction. We don't worry about it, because if a major attack occurs, we'll be killed instantly. Surviving a nuclear attack would be far worse. Downwind Texas, for example, should be quite worried about the radiation.

Working in an emergency department as a risk researcher, after my previous ER encounters and friendships with emergency physician climbing partners, felt ironic. My respect increased for ER docs and nurses, who have one of the most difficult jobs I can imagine. They were also a fascinating bunch from a risk perspective. They worked risky jobs in a chaotic and risky environment, yet many were also climbers, skiers, kayakers, and so on. Edgeworkers, indeed.

My position didn't last long due to funding issues, so I ended up back in environmental work to pay the bills. Much of the work involved radioactive waste disposal. Teams of scientists and statisticians worked together as seers to predict the future of buried waste and human society thousands of years into the future. This predictive computer modeling was complex and interesting, but we might as well have donned pointy hats and robes and gathered around a crystal ball. The public's fear of radiation drove the work, but trust me, there are much worse things to worry about.

Shortly after we moved, on a spring approach to climb some rarely formed ice couloirs near the Santa Fe ski area, Linda confessed, "I just don't want to do this any longer." She had shoulder surgery shortly before moving. Along with her new job, it contributed to her retirement from technical climbing. Her revelation was a shock, but I should've seen it coming. My immediate thought was "Wow, does this mean divorce?" According to Linda, I ranted for a while. That was silly, but we'd been climbing together for a quarter century, so it took a while for me to adjust. My main climbing-addiction partner had moved on.

I'd been climbing with Linda and a few others with similar attitudes toward risk for many years. Most of the dudes from whom I learned climbing risk management were pros and mountain guides. I was therefore appalled at some of the risky mountain traveler attitudes I encountered after I returned to the US, in Colorado in particular. I could fill this account with horror-shows, but I'll describe a few incidents that contributed to my eventual retirement from technical climbing. The rewards started to take a back seat to human-factor risks.

There are a few alpine routes in New Mexico, and a lot of rock climbing, but Colorado has much more, and lots of ice. We bought the Durango home as a weekend bivi. Most of my climbing was in the southwestern part of the state, home to much of the good alpine and ice climbing. The climbing in Colorado isn't nearly on the same compelling scale as the Canadian Rockies, but there's a lot of it.

The Colorado *14ers*, the state's 14,000-plus-foot peaks, attract a group of interesting goal-seekers. There are more than fifty 14ers, and crowds of hikers seek to bag all of them. The main appeal is nearly all the peaks have non-technical routes. The starting plateau is also high, so the base-to-peak vertical distances aren't as great as many other ranges. Many peaks are just big humps with wide trails to the summit, and people and dogs run up and down.

Once baggers bag all the 14ers, they have almost six-hundred 13ers to bag. Some are more difficult by the easiest route than any 14er. A few people have even gone further and bagged the almost seven-hundred 12ers, which bags the question: Don't these baggers have to work? Some turn the 14ers into a race course, or they climb them all in winter, or they climb them all naked. Okay, the last one probably hasn't been done—yet.

This arbitrary, altitude goal-seeking phenomenon isn't limited to Colorado. Scotland has the Munros, for example. However, the phenomenon has resulted in a situation in which Colorado hikers without technical experience put themselves at types of risk often restricted to experienced climbers. There's an additional impetus to summit, given the summit tick list. I'm not in any way suggesting these folks shouldn't climb 14ers, but many, in my observation, aren't thinking like risk managers. All mountains are dangerous, after all.

Our dogs and I once hiked the 14er Mt. Belford in an autumn whiteout and squall of horizontal graupel. As we were ascending, a gentleman of my advanced age in jeans, a cotton flannel shirt, old soaked rain jacket, and running shoes stumbled and slipped down the icy trail. He cautioned it was "dangerous up there." I want to somehow broadcast a message to the entire world: *Dammit, all mountains are dangerous!*

He claimed to have crawled to the summit, due to the high winds. He lied. Fresh snow blanketed the summit with no tracks aside from those of our dogs, who had preceded me. I wonder whether he included Belford on his tick list? The old duffer was putting himself in danger, regardless. He seemed slow, inexperienced and was dressed in cotton *death fabric,* which soaks up water and becomes useless as insulation, but he apparently didn't know any better.

I don't know if any hikers have died to date doing this sort of thing on 14ers. Good accident reports and statistics don't exist for Colorado outside of possibly Rocky Mountain National Park, but I'd expect deaths and injuries have and will continue to happen.

During a trip in which I climbed the 14ers Snowmass Mountain and Capitol Peak, I observed numerous cases of dangerous behavior on the part of 14er-ers. Afterward, I posted what I thought was an educational discussion and recommendations from a climber's perspective on a popular website. I described ways hikers might want to educate themselves in climbing equipment and techniques, risk management, and wilderness travel. With this knowledge, they could at least climb the more difficult peaks efficiently and safely. Few Americans undergo formal training for mountaineering, and there's no regulation or certification process like some other dangerous sports. Any jackleg dirtbag can buy a rope and some pro and go climbing.

I was taken aback by the largely negative reaction to my posting. Some technical climbers supported me, but they were a minority. I was viciously flamed, and a common theme seemed to be "I just didn't understand" 14er-ers. The flamers claimed they didn't need to know anything about climbing or safe wilderness travel, even on more technical peaks. It was disturbing. I truly don't understand why hikers want to put themselves at undue risk by not learning to think like climbers or risk managers.

It was also perplexing to read discussions on the website regarding, for example, the best pistols to carry while ascending 14ers. I've seen people packing sidearms on several. It could be a political statement. Some people on the website asked why the packers want to pack, and a typical response was, "It's my right." That's true, but it's also their right to hike up a peak in a snowstorm wearing death fabric and running shoes. Doesn't mean it's a good idea.

There should be a practical reason for carrying any equipment, in light of *light-is-right*. A loaded pistol is heavy. Perhaps the pistol-packers are afraid of bears or other animals. If so, they don't seem to be aware that handguns are useless against such aggressive animals. I've yet to see any large animals to worry about on any of the 14ers. If the packers are afraid, bear spray is more effective, lighter than a gun, and doesn't require extensive practice.

The joke in Alaska is the best use of a pistol in a bear attack is to shoot your partner in the knee, and run like hell.

Linda and I lost interest in Colorado peaks over 14,000 feet due to crowding, except maybe for off-season hikes or ski trips. It's a shame, as many are outstanding peaks, and combinations of several in the same day are often possible. In contrast, we've been on many shorter peaks without another soul in sight, although this may change as more and more people continue their tick-tick-ticking beyond the 14ers.

I was fortunate to climb with some good New Mexican and Coloradan partners, but some were downright scary. I never encountered such climbing partners in the Cascades or Canada, but perhaps this was random luck. It was difficult to tell until I got out there.

There was the guy who didn't want to wear his helmet in a steep snow couloir where numerous rocks were zipping past because, he said, "It's too hot." Or the dude whose eyes were bigger than his stomach, and who wimped out in the middle of an easy but committing traverse, forcing us to rap down crappy loose terrain with extensive rockfall. I assumed partners would practice basic risk management and check out the characteristics of a route beforehand, including length, difficulty, and so on. Apparently, this was a presumption on my part and too much to ask.

Some tried to argue with me with regard to route-finding, despite the fact I had a couple of decades' worth of experience on them in successful wilderness and climbing route-finding, including a decade of surveying experience. One of the few things I can do well is navigate in the mountains. Sorry, but I'm not going to put myself and others at risk by deferring to a relative newbie with regard to which bloody way to go. I'll defer to pro mountain guides, but in some cases, I've even questioned them.

Ice climbing in Colorado is downright dangerous, the greatest risk being other people. It's not advisable to climb any ice route with another party ahead, which Linda and I learned on Polar Circus. It applies particularly to narrow gullies or pillars, as opposed to big walls of ice such as the Weeping Wall in the Canadian Rockies. In Canada, if a car was in the parking area near a climb, we hopped back in our car and drove for a few minutes to find a climb to ourselves.

This often isn't possible in Colorado; there are just too many people. Unless we were first on a route, we had to accept being hit by ice. Sometimes it just made us laugh, as on the beautiful and popular climb Stairway to Heaven. Not only ice chunks whizzed past our heads, but also a glove, a screw, and a small camera.

The ice climbing can be good in Colorado, but the temperature typically doesn't stay cold in the winter like the Canadian Rockies. Freeze-thaw cycles can result in horrible layered and incohesive ice. I soloed the nine-hundred foot Whorehouse Hoses on ice requiring a lot of cleaning to get good tool plants. It looked like I'd shot the thing with a large caliber automatic weapon, due to the holes I dug. It was exhausting, but I maintained. When I returned to the parking lot, a ski guide who was organizing a back-country trip asked what I'd done, and his reply was "Sick!" Sick, indeed.

One of the most dicey situations I've ever been in while ice climbing was at the top of an unprotectable pitch in Kennedy Gully, when the crappy thin ice ran out altogether and I was forced to delicately dry-tool about ten feet up on a steep, featureless wet rock slab to a belay ledge. If I'd been able to see from below this was going to happen, I wouldn't have launched off on it at all. I would've fallen over a hundred feet and likely died if I'd lost it.

Colorado can have nasty and sometimes barely predictable avalanche risk, applicable to both climbs and ski slopes. One spring, Linda and I backcountry skied above Silverton, following a bunch of snowmobile and ski tracks up to a ridge above timberline. We went slightly off the main track and felt a big *whummmp*. A weak snow layer had collapsed over a large area. This isn't necessarily a sign of imminent avalanche, but it usually isn't good. We dug a quick diagnostic snow pit which revealed several weak layers. No other pits were evident. A lot of snowmobilers and skiers were lucky the slope they were ascending didn't slide. We turned around, gingerly skied down, and enjoyed a nice coffee in Silverton.

Backcountry skiing in Colorado and elsewhere has exploded in popularity, due to a combination of population growth and improvements in equipment. Similar influences apply to snowmobiling as well. There are many more uneducated skiers and snowmobilers in the wintry Colorado hills compared to ten years ago.

Some backcountry skiers seem to think because they're skilled at turning and able to ski steep runs at resorts, this qualifies them to safely ski in the backcountry. They often seem to forget their helmets. They must think a rescue transceiver will magically protect them from avalanches. I've seen some wearing transceivers outside their clothing where they will instantly get ripped off in a slide. Some don't have shovels, or they have tiny plastic ones that would be useless for rapidly digging somebody out of a slide.

Crowding and human-factor risks in the US began to outweigh the rewards I gained from technical climbing. I found climbing to be highly rewarding, so this provides an indication of the severity of the risks. It's possible that American Rockies climbers who don't have extensive experiences in other areas don't realize they climb in such risky conditions, but I had such non-American experiences. Human-factor risks are high in other crowded areas such as the Alps, but at least in the Alps, there's generally expert and efficient rescue available. This isn't the case in most of the Rockies. Crowding and human-factor risks have also caused me to lose interest in backcountry skiing, in more popular areas. It's still possible to find solitude in the American Rockies, but it's increasingly difficult.

Another contributor to my climbing retirement was a positive experience. This was the Grand Traverse of the major Teton peaks surrounding the Grand Teton. It's a fantastic link-up of multiple technical peaks, one of the best in the US. It involves about 25,000 feet of elevation gain and loss, over eighteen miles of largely technical terrain.

I hired Max, a senior mountain guide. He was a cool cat indeed, who sported a ponytail, drove a VW microbus, and carried a hemp chalk bag. There were a few pitches I wouldn't have wanted to lead *on-sight* or lead without knowing what they were like. I also suspected the route-finding was complex, which was indeed true. Further, it was a record snow year in the Tetons, and even in mid-July, a large amount of snow and ice blanketed the range. People were still ski mountaineering. Even though Max had led this traverse more than ten times, he hadn't done it in such alpine conditions.

When dry, this would have been a pure rock traverse that may have taken us twenty hours or less. Instead, it took three long days with two planned bivis, moving continuously and fast. At least the hardest rock pitches, for example on the North Ridge of the Grand Teton, were mostly free of ice and snow. The bivis were cold and uncomfortable in our tiny tent and thin sleeping bags. We schlepped our bivi gear over many peaks and thousands of feet of technical terrain. Light-was-right, but unpleasant in actual use. It was also windy at night, so every time I'd drift off to sleep, the tent started flapping and spanked me in the ass or face, depending on which way I assed or faced. I didn't get a lot of sleep.

We encountered a grizzly on the hike out. We saw nobody the entire time except at the hut at the base of the dog route on the Grand and on the hike out. I loved it all. It was one of the high points of my mountaineering life.

However, I was starting to feel a bit old for this sort of stuff, if I wasn't willing to put in the time and effort of continuous training. I was fifty-five. It was harder to stay fit and took longer to recover as I aged, and I couldn't move as fast as I could in my forties. Hell, the fortyish guide Max looked wiped out, and he did this for a living. Plenty of people my age at the time and older are still out there, banging out the routes, but they train and climb a lot more than I did. When I sent photos of the jaunt to a non-climber friend, he asked, "Why do you push yourself so hard?" The answer was, "Because I can." I started to realize, though, perhaps I no longer could.

I've known climbers to retire due to accidents, physical injury, cumulative fear, having children, and so on. Nobody can keep climbing forever. Linda and I both simply lost the love for technical climbing, if not for each other. The upsides no longer outweighed the downsides. Our criterion of climbing novel aesthetic alpine and ice routes all by our lonesome selves became more and more difficult to achieve over time.

We were spoiled by climbing in pristine areas during a time when the hills weren't as crowded. It was also increasingly difficult to balance climbing and our jobs, which Linda felt earlier than me. The type of climbing we did took a lot out of us, physically and mentally.

We enjoyed a great quarter century of alpine, rock, and ice climbing together. It was enough. Linda and I still scramble up peaks on which other climbers may or may not use a rope. My last roped climb in 2013 was an easy ice climb called Goldrush near Silverton, with two friends. This was shortly before my fifty-seventh birthday. I retired from work a few years later, largely due to physical issues preventing me from working long hours at a desk, but I was also weary of thinking about risk in a professional capacity.

A positive aspect of climbing retirement is we have enough high-quality warm clothing and boots to last us until we die. We aren't wearing the stuff out nearly as fast. I donated my rock gear to a local mountain rescue organization. You'll have to pry my ice tools from my cold, dead hands, though. Those things helped to take me places I never would've believed even existed as a youth. I also kept a few ropes. Rope is always handy.

Many older climbers start doing more sport or gym climbing, which bore me to tears. Others start trail running, or mountain biking. My hat's off to these folks, but both are subject to injuries and chronic musculoskeletal damage, which I don't need more of at my age. Skiing continues to interest us, but backcountry skiing is contingent on uncrowded and stable snow conditions. Lift-served, heli, and cat skiing are expensive. So, skiing satisfies my outdoor and risk jones only to a limited extent.

Linda bought me a wonderful combined 2012 Christmas and birthday present as a salve to my risk jones, thirty laps at the Phoenix International Raceway in a "Drive Petty" six-hundred horsepower Dodge stock car. She kept the details secret, telling me only that we were flying to Phoenix, but I'd love it. Phoenix isn't my favorite destination, so this gift was a real mystery. I was never a fan of auto racing, but I did like to drive fast back in the day. Coincidentally, Richard Petty grew up not far from me in North Carolina. If I'd known back then I could've become a multi-millionaire driving cars fast, I may have taken an entirely different life path.

As opposed to the barely controllable brutes of the past, the Dodge was the safest car I've ever driven. A driver could run it into a wall at high speed and jump out laughing. No ABS or airbags in sight. I wish all cars were designed this way, but I suppose they'd be expensive, and many drivers would object to crawling through the open window and other discomforts. At first, the experience was rather weird, but by the last ten laps, I was laughing with glee, without running it into a wall. Not something I'll likely repeat, but it was a blast to do once.

Linda has focused more on work, and other outdoor activities have served as climbing replacements for us, although they're not necessarily as risky. Rediscovering the joys of hiking itself is one replacement. To typical climbers, a hike is something they have to suffer through to get to a climb; literally, called an "approach." As climbers, we enjoyed many of these hikes, and loathed others, but the hike itself wasn't the thing. We've returned to our roots, if not our routes.

Another replacement has been adopting smart athletic dogs who're capable of wilderness travel, and love it. Linda and I occasionally hiked with our previous dogs, but as we climbed more often, they had to stay home most of the time. No longer.

Hiking with dogs gives us a different perspective on the natural world. Dogs experience it chiefly via odor and hearing. They don't seem to care much about the visual world, unless an animal is moving. Their level of raw athleticism is so far beyond human it's thrilling, and makes us question the evolutionary wisdom of humans abandoning four-legged locomotion. It's a joy to see sixty pounds of canine muscle, after hiking many miles and summiting a 14er, run full out at 13,000 feet for a quarter mile over steep terrain. Our dogs can cruise up easy technical slabs with no problem, as long as there's good friction.

Not all people are thrilled by dogs in the wilderness, and many are even afraid of them. There are books and classes for such people to deal with their fears. Dogs have been a symbiotic partner of humans since domestication many thousands of years ago. Humans should be in charge, but if they watch and listen to what dogs try to communicate and there's mutual respect, the dogs will love them without qualification and the humans will learn much.

Linda and I are now in the *de facto* role of hiking guides who manage risks to our furry family members. It amazes me to see petite people far out in the backcountry with a ninety or hundred-pound dog they could never hope to carry out if it were injured, or dogs who are fat and unfit. Few trail runners with dogs carry doggie first aid kits. I don't see many who carry anything aside from a phone and a small water bottle. They seem to forget dogs need a lot of water and have to pant to avoid hyperthermia rather than the more efficient human sweating.

Few if any pro rescuers will risk human lives and expend resources rescuing a pet, so how ready and willing are owners to perform doggie rescue? We carry a small light tarp, for example, and can use trekking poles to rig a litter if need be. Toting even a twenty-pound dog out any distance ain't easy.

The riskiest activities we've done post-climbing likely involve hiking with dogs in large-animal territory, such as the Wind River Range and the Canadian Rockies. We once backpacked into the Wind Rivers and belatedly found we were camping near a wolf den, judging by their howls later in the night. The dogs went on alert but stayed cool.

Some dog breeds are not afraid of large animals, so we have to keep them under tight voice control. We rarely use leashes. This is especially important if we're in large-animal country, and can't see what lies ahead due to brush or other obstacles. A dog who pisses off a bear, for example, puts everyone at risk. Linda and I protect ourselves and our dogs using careful risk management and by carrying bear spray. Good dogs will defend their owners to the death, and it's worth keeping their noble loyalty in mind.

A great attribute of the Southwest desert is the ease of finding solitude. We've taken the dogs to isolated areas of the Sandia Mountain foothills near Albuquerque well over two thousand mornings, and rarely see other people. The desert, however, has its own risks. Heat can be managed by not going out during mid-day. The dogs have learned to run from shade to shade. Lack of water is a problem, and it's good we no longer climb—water is damn heavy to carry. Rattlesnakes and coyotes, as well as bear and cougar in the higher areas, pose risks largely to the dogs.

Some people pose risks to both dogs and owners. I've heard of dogs being pepper-sprayed, which I wouldn't take kindly to at all. I've been yelled at and stink-eyed a few times for no apparent reason—unexpected, given the large number of current and retired military personnel in Albuquerque, and the prevalence of people carrying firearms. Perhaps the yellers and stink-eyers reckon I'm too old to open up a can of whup-ass. They're probably right, so I just smile and keep on truckin'.

Cactus spines are a constant, though minor problem. The dogs have learned to let me extract them, after getting spines stuck in their lips and tongues from trying to remove the spines themselves. My legs are scratched and pricked on a continuous basis. I'll sometimes discover large spines in my skin while showering or lying in bed.

In the remote desert country of New Mexico and Utah, the greatest risk might be getting stuck or lost. Flat tires are common at trailheads, due to ubiquitous broken glass. I've considered lobbying to have beer bottle glass designated the State Mineral of New Mexico. The terrain and the route-finding can be highly complex. Finding the area of interest while driving complex networks of 4WD roads, and not getting stuck, can be challenging. If a driver goes off the beaten path, some of these areas are as remote as any found in the lower forty-eight states. It's enormously expensive to tow vehicles great distances if they become stuck. Sometimes this isn't even possible for several days, especially if it rains heavily and roads turn to mud.

Linda, Paul, and I were once trapped while hiking on the wrong side of the Dirty Devil River in southern Utah after it rained for three days, and the placid shallow river we'd previously skipped across was an impassible Dirty Devil. I have photos of red mud waterfalls cascading down the canyon walls. Once we were able to cross the raging, thigh-deep river a day after it stopped raining, we slithered out along thirty miles of muddy roads and washouts in a rented white 4WD. It was painted completely red with mud when we returned it. Shockingly, they didn't charge us for cleaning. After this, I became much more cautious as to where and when I drove in the desert. Mud is nasty.

Linda and I find it interesting and challenging to hike off-trail in complex desert terrain, without GPS and often without a detailed map, and make it back to the truck without issues. We've been able to explore many areas rarely or never trod by human or canine feet. Traveling safely in psychedelic desert terrain like no other on Earth, with nobody else for miles, is highly rewarding. I won't reveal specifics, as I want these areas to remain undiscovered by others.

Being able to carry a real camera again provides a creative outlet that partially substitutes for risk. I carried a film camera body and multiple lenses before Linda and I started climbing. When we were climbing, carrying the extra weight was painful, and often it just wasn't feasible to carry more than a little point-and-shoot. Hiking without excess climbing nylon and metal allows me to carry a better camera and take my time composing photos.

A major creative outlet for me is music. I'd played a lot in Chapel Hill, and a little in Seattle and Calgary, but it's difficult to play both inside and outside while working full-time. After retirement, I had more time for music. I found superb music-mates even in the musical desert of Albuquerque.

I learned digital recording and production, and—with the dudes I'd found—jointly produced more than a thousand recorded improvisational jazz and rock pieces. A non-musician neighbor described our music this way: "I don't understand what you are doing, but it sounds as if you know what you are doing." I took it as a compliment. I flowed on a nearly-every-week basis. I doubt I'll ever experience such a creative group collaboration again. Improvisation is the LSD of music.

Weirdly, I've even started writing prose and poetry. Perhaps the act of creativity is a cognitive substitute for the rewards associated with risk management. Both require an extreme focus necessary for my mental health. Seems to be working so far. The next stage of my life, in which I'll no doubt become less physically active, will likely focus even more on creativity. At least that's what I'm aiming for. Meditation, for example, may fulfill my need for flow and focus, but if I can create music, prose and poetry, then why not?

Albuquerque has many creative and top-tier tattoo artists. Some of their work is truly beautiful. When I started playing music regularly, I felt rather naked compared to the heavily inked dudes I was jamming with. I decided to get some tats, and I wasn't even a stoner.

I located an artist whose work I admired. When I showed up for my appointment, the first thing I asked the heavily inked and pierced young receptionist was, "Could you run me through your sterilization procedures, and general approach to avoiding infection?" He seemed flustered, and called in the owner, who was even more heavily inked and pierced. He gave me a full and detailed rundown. He told me nobody had ever asked about infection risk before. I didn't find that surprising, even though improper procedures can result in bacterial infections, or worse, viral infections such as HIV. It would be difficult to track adverse outcomes, aside from possible regret, as a result of tattoos. Most people just don't view risk through the same lens I use. Their sterilization process seemed fine, and I experienced no health problems.

Linda and I've both suffered multiple medical errors since we returned to the US. A particularly painful and potentially lethal event involved my scrotum again. I developed a scrotal cyst, which initially pleased me. It appeared as if I sported three testicles just like Dr. Evil in the *Austin Powers* movies, but the cyst became uncomfortable. It was removed once, with no substantial issues, but the bastard grew back. What should've been a routine and simple second surgery turned into a bleeding nightmare. My blood-filled scrotum expanded to the size of a grapefruit, yet it took hours for me to be seen in the crowded ER.

Similar to the shingles incident, it was a classic case study of errors and delays. I wrote it up as a medical system analysis and published it in a medical journal. Everything is still urologically functional, but it was a close call. My advice is to stay out of the medical system as much as possible, particularly the US medical system. All hospitals, like all mountains, are dangerous. If Linda hadn't been there, I could've easily died a truly unpleasant death. If the health system door must be entered, make sure somebody responsible like Linda accompanies you as your risk management advocate.

Between pitches on my first climb of Whorehouse Hoses, near Silverton, Colorado. Note the screamers with carabiners, typically used on crappy ice. I soloed this climb at a later date, and the ice was still crappy (credit: K. Craig).

The top of Kennedy Gully, near Ouray, Colorado, with the highway far below. I led this thin ice pitch, culminating with the smooth wet rock to my partner's right. His expression seems to say "WTF?" (credit: R. C. Lee).

My last roped climb in 2013: Goldrush, near Silverton, Colorado. There are blood-stains on my green gloves from my previous lip-splitting episode in Alberta (credit: K. Craig)

I'm fondling the safest car I've ever driven, in Phoenix, Arizona (credit: L. Cook).

Our rescue dogs Jasper (Tennessee Brindle), Lindo (Plott Hound), and I on Mt. Wheeler, New Mexico. Jasper climbed Mt. Wheeler for the first time, in the snow, when he was less than one year old (credit: R. C. Lee).

Losing myself taking photos in the Dali-esque landscape of the Rio Puerco valley, New Mexico (credit: L. Cook).

A retired climber, creating and recording the experience (credit: T. Ravenhawk).

Coda

I BACKPACK TO A REMOTE AREA OF THE NORTH CASCADES. I WANDER OFF-trail from camp. While taking photos of the spectacular views, I stumble upon an ancient circle of rocks next to a tarn, almost hidden by wild blueberries and other alpine plants. In the center is a bear skull partially buried in the tundra. Later, I describe what I saw to a knowledgeable friend, who informs me it was a Native American vision quest site, given the particular location. It's the only explanation, given the apparent age of the artifacts. Its builder was seeking a door.

❦

My life has been a series of quests, not seeking visions or supernatural experience, but transformative doorways, flow states, and connections to different states of consciousness as well as to the natural world itself. The wellspring of experience, for me, is the edge. I've been close to the edge through focused cognitive and physical exploration in high-risk conditions, thousands of times, alone and with partners. Risk is an essential ingredient in much of what I consider to be worthwhile.

I recently saw the documentary *Amazing Grace* with the great Aretha Franklin. Listening to her sing, like no other, the traditional gospel song "Climbing Higher Mountains," I busted out in tears. I've been climbing mountains, metaphorical and corporeal, my entire life, trying to get home.

I've been an edgeworker or risk management addict since I was young, running barefoot among the snakes and climbing rock solo. It's possible my father instilled in me both a genetic and a behavioral tendency to seek out and enter risky doors—but to manage risks to the fullest extent possible. I was subject to involuntary risk when I was young, growing up malnourished in a single-parent household with a mother who suffered from mental illness and drug abuse, in a local culture steeped in toxic racism and a contaminated environment. This youth may have contributed to my desire to manage risks. The losses associated with some of those risks followed me for years, even to the present day. I don't know how I would've developed differently if, for example, I'd grown up in a loving two-parent household in a liberal, wealthy urban environment.

I recently had a climbing dream, which is rare. I climbed a loose, vertical route on a rock tower, rising from a vast plain. As I downclimbed a convoluted descent route, I fell a great distance and landed on a ledge, unhurt. I stood up and continued to figure out the route. I ran across the plain, and encountered a raging river. I pondered this a bit, and ran across it. I felt no fear at all during this dream. I just worked the problem and derived a solution. I think like a risk manager, even in my sleep. Perhaps it's been beaten into me.

I don't regret my voluntarily risky life path at all. It's been an interesting and rewarding ride, and I could die tomorrow a happy dude. My lifestyle isn't for everybody, but it worked for me. For me, growing old and the simple act of waking up each morning are profoundly rewarding.

My life was and still is subject to involuntary and voluntary risks, but many people lead lives subject to extreme risk. Firefighters, police, and emergency medical personnel are exposed to constant danger. Rodeo riding, big-wave surfing, parasailing, cave diving, and extreme skiing are perilous sports. Many criminals live under extreme legal and personal risk. Anybody who lives or works in a conflict zone or under a repressive regime suffers daily risk. Millions of people live in the shadow of active volcanoes, or in hurricane or typhoon zones.

Many folks don't appear to realize they live risky lives. They don't consider driving to be dangerous, and indeed distract themselves while driving by texting and other means. Combinations of common voluntary risk factors, such as alcohol and nicotine use, eating lots of sugar and fatty foods, an indolent lifestyle, and motorcycle riding result in a greatly increased probability of premature death. Lots of individuals would likely live longer, healthier lives if they thought about their own cumulative risk.

Although my life may not have been as risky as some, it's been packed with a wide range of risky situations over six decades. I've had the vantage of being a scientist who has spent those decades thinking hard about risk in his work and most aspects of life. I find risk fascinating, but some people have asked me how I sleep at night. I sleep just fine. I'd much rather know what's going to hit me and be able to do something about it than to not think about it and hope for the best. Ignoring risk doesn't make it go away.

⁓

I did a lot of technical climbing. However, I wasn't a famous badass climber by any means. I didn't make many first ascents, and I didn't climb 8,000-meter peaks. I wasn't featured in climbing magazines, and I'm not on the motivational speaker circuit. I estimate that I led or soloed over ninety percent of the technical climbs I completed, but that's probably due to my unusual climbing history.

Many amazing mountains and routes allowed me to climb them, and I'm grateful. I was addicted to climbing and found it rewarding for many years, as did Linda. Climbing, however, took a back seat to being a decent husband and a good scientist, having a productive scientific career with positive personal and social impacts, and creating art and music.

My views on climbing risk differ from those of many accomplished and well-published climbers who aren't risk scientists. For example, I read a recent perspective on risk management published by a major climbing organization. It was so simplistic I laughed out loud. Simple approaches to risk management may be fine in some cases, but most climbing involves a complex and dynamic set of risks. In my view, these should be managed carefully while acknowledging the complexity and changes over time. Many climbers simply think differently than I do. I approached climbing risk management with as much thought and care as I did in any of my professional risk work; if not more so, considering the downsides of not managing the risks.

Linda and I took and still take Dirty Harry's philosophy seriously: "Man's got to know his limitations," good, non-gender-specific advice. To our minds, this is an essential component of risk management in the mountains, or anywhere. We never attempted climbs that we thought we wouldn't be able to pull off and get back home alive. To do otherwise, would have been irrational.

At a past Society for Risk Analysis conference dinner, I was relating one of the innumerable climbing stories residing in my head. I was taken aback when a scientist sitting at my table, a man I didn't know, opined that climbing is irresponsible. When I asked in what way, he pointed to the societal costs of climbing, such as rescues. I replied, "I make every effort to avoid rescue, I've never been rescued, and I carry rescue insurance." He brought up personal costs, the prospect of death. I replied, "My wife is my usual climbing partner, her level of risk aversion is similar to mine, we have no children, and we carry a lot of life insurance." He persisted and became agitated by my risk-scientist answers, but thankfully the conversation shifted to a less controversial subject.

Even as a fellow scientist, he couldn't accept the way I think about risk. I don't disagree with the proposition that climbing is irrational, but risks in irrational activities can be managed in a rational fashion. Although I may not have convinced him, my argument doesn't involve rationalization in the usual sense of the word. Rather, it's a reasonable way to deal with a dangerous activity and stay alive. I don't know what my other risk colleagues think of me and my activities, but I hope they have confidence I think hard about risk, especially when conducting activities that could kill me.

My brain chemistry and psychology have likely changed as a result of numerous pharmacological influences, contributing to greater freedom of thought and expression. There may have been downsides. I doubt, however, I've suffered as much organic brain damage as many people my age who have taken legal prescription anticholinergics and benzodiazepines for years, or consumed a lot of alcohol, or subjected themselves to combinations of many legal but toxic substances.

My body has suffered. I may have suffered mild concussions from bonking my head or getting it bonked, but I can't remember. The cumulative physical damage wrought by decades of physical work and sport isn't trivial, and chronic pain will haunt me for the rest of my life unless great advances are made in the science of pain management. I'm not sure many athletes think about long-term physical damage when they're young. I know climbers and skiers in their thirties who have already experienced multiple injuries and surgeries that will affect them the rest of their lives. I'm not implying they shouldn't climb or ski, but they should be aware they'll have to live with the pain and reduced function for decades. This is one reason

I'm content I didn't start technical climbing and skiing until I was relatively old. I never thought I was invincible, and I tried to manage the injuries I suffered so I could continue climbing and skiing.

Sitting at a desk, however, has had the worst effect on my body, and indeed contributed to my early work retirement. I'm glad I'm finished with work. My stress level was high from struggling with the irrational approaches to risk practiced by many people, organizations, and government agencies. The only minor regret I have is that I didn't study risk psychology. Unscientific and irrational views of risk as well as the emotional response of fear itself are perhaps the greatest challenges humanity faces.

Risk itself has become politicized; many on the right end of the spectrum believe those on the left are concerned about the wrong risks or even fabricate them, and vice versa. This is nonsensical. Risk is politically agnostic. Unless humans get over their fears and start viewing and managing risk through the lens of science and reason, they'll suffer mightily. Studying a problem and doing something about it are two different things. Had I studied the psychology of risk, maybe I'd feel as if I'd made more of a contribution to this pressing problem.

Regardless, I have a thick resume, and I feel proud of the majority of my body of work. Publications were the *summits* of consulting and academic *climbs*. In a few cases, I made a difference and saved lives; for example, in the worlds of medical risk management and the prevention of catastrophic events. I've also tried to educate others in risk analysis and management, in my work and otherwise. Hopefully, some of it stuck.

These are seriously risky times. Don't believe the famous authors and pundits who claim life has never been better. They need a good risk education. Climate change, overpopulation, war, bigotry, political instability, terrorism, propaganda, social media, and similar risks need to be taken seriously and quickly addressed. Time is running out, fast.

In late 2019, vast destructive fires burned across the US West. The COVID-19 global pandemic infected tens of millions of people and damaged economies around the world in 2020, and is ongoing at the time of this writing. A violent insurrection occurred against the US government in early 2021. These events are appalling examples of risk management failures. Yet, many people seem to think society can just carry on as usual and "get back to normal." I seriously doubt it. These and other large-scale risk management failures are a wakeup call. There's a high probability we'll all be thrown violently back into a hellish, pre-Industrial Age world, absent strong action and substantial change. No sane person would allow this collapse to happen.

Much of my life has been hampered by financial hardship, but things could've been much more challenging. Random luck resulted in me being born a somewhat-intelligent White male in North America during a relatively placid and prosperous period in history. I was fortunate to have the freedom to lead a risky life, to possess the physical and mental abilities to do risky stuff, and to build a career focused on risk. My life and career could've been boring, and this memoir wouldn't have been written.

Freedom's a wonderful thing. Apologies to Mr. Kristofferson, but freedom ain't just another word for nothing left to lose. I hope we Americans don't lose our freedom due to selfishness, greed, stupidity, and lack of critical thinking. I agree with John Stuart Mill: "The only freedom which deserves the name is that of pursuing our own good, in our own way, so long as we do not attempt to deprive others of theirs, or impede their efforts to obtain it." Many Americans ignore the latter part of Mill's philosophy, at their own peril.

I was also fortunate, in an admittedly selfish sense, to have lived during a time in which outdoor recreation was limited to a small percentage of the population. Every wild area wasn't guide-booked, blogged, or selfied to death. There aren't many secrets left. My uncertain risk journey was worthwhile, and wilderness provided and still provides a degree of sanity.

In addition to the many other ways in which I've been fortunate in my long, risky life, the absolute summit of fortune was finding a mate and able partner in opening dangerous doors. Linda is the blackest positive swan in my life experience. I don't believe in gods, but if I did, I'd be on my knees every day in thankful prayer. Whatever future risks arise, I feel confident Linda and I can manage them together. No worthwhile doors are closed to us. I hope others find such superb partners in life and risk.

Acknowledgements

I WROTE THE FIRST DRAFT OF THIS MEMOIR IN 2019, SHORTLY AFTER I retired from work. Not only is Linda my capable risk and life partner, but she suffered through many readings of drafts and offered editorial advice. Andrea Lee (no relation) from Albuquerque read an initial draft and provided editorial suggestions. My siblings and a few friends commented on the accuracy of particular sections. Our fine hounds, Jasper and Lindo, provided endless amusement and distraction from writing. My bandmates Yobs in the Snicket provided an astoundingly creative and productive musical outlet.

I wouldn't have been able to climb many technical routes without capable partners, in addition to Linda, and professional mountain guides. We all had many stimulating conversations about mountains and risk management. Several individuals provided life-changing employment opportunities and education. Many scientists and nonscientists helped me think about risk in general, and provided intellectual stimulus over the years. All y'all know who y'all are, and I thank y'all profusely. Thanks also to the many health professionals who have kept my body active and working.

Finally, thank you to the professional WiDo team who gave me the chance to publish this memoir and helped craft it into a better story. Special thanks to Karen Gowen, whose careful editorial advice was invaluable.

About the Author

Robert Charles Lee is a retired risk scientist with over twenty-five years of academic and applied risk analysis, decision analysis, and risk management experi-  ence. He and his wife Linda have climbed hundreds of technical and non-technical mountain, rock, ice, and canyon routes, and hiked thousands of miles in several countries. Lee is also an avid musician and photographer.

For more information, please visit https://robertcharleslee.com.

CPSIA information can be obtained
at www.ICGtesting.com
Printed in the USA
FSHW020208210721
83302FS